KW-222-228

Contents

100592906

BUILDING SUSTAINABLE HOUSING MARKETS

333.
3322
BUi

BUILDING SUSTAINABLE HOUSING MARKETS

Lessons from a decade of changing demand and Housing Market Renewal

Ed Ferrari and Peter Lee

Chartered Institute of Housing Practice Studies

in collaboration with

the Housing Studies Association

The Chartered Institute of Housing

The Chartered Institute of Housing (CIH) is the professional body for people involved in housing and communities. We are a registered charity and not-for-profit organisation. We have a diverse and growing membership of over 21,000 people – both in the public and private sectors – living and working in over 20 countries on five continents across the world. We exist to maximise the contribution that housing professionals make to the wellbeing of communities. Our vision is to be the first point of contact for – and the credible voice of – anyone involved or interested in housing.

Chartered Institute of Housing
Octavia House, Westwood Way, Coventry CV4 8JP
Tel: 024 7685 1700
Email: customer.services@cih.org
Website: www.cih.org

The Housing Studies Association

The Housing Studies Association promotes the study of housing by bringing together housing researchers with others interested in housing research in the housing policy and practitioner communities. It acts as a voice for housing research by organising conferences and seminars, lobbying government and other agencies and providing services to members.

The CIH Housing Practice Studies are published in collaboration with the Housing Studies Association and aim to provide important and valuable material and insights for housing managers, staff, students, trainers and policy-makers. Books in the series are designed to promote debate, but the contents do not necessarily reflect the views of the CIH or the HSA. The Editorial Team for the series is: General Editors: Dr. Peter Williams, John Perry and Ed Ferrari, and Production Editor: Alan Dearling.

Cover photographs: Places for People

ISBN: 978-1-905018-27-7

Building sustainable housing markets: Lessons from a decade of changing demand and Housing Market Renewal
Ed Ferrari and Peter Lee

Published by the Chartered Institute of Housing
© 2010
Printed on FSC stock from sustainable sources by Hobbs the Printers Ltd, Totton, Hampshire SO40 3WX

List of figures

List of tables

Acknowledgements

The original thoughts and drafting for this volume on Housing Market Renewal were conducted back in the autumn of 2005 and we originally envisaged this to be an assessment of how we arrived at the problems of low demand and an early evaluation of HMR interventions. As we developed the ideas for the book our perspectives changed and the events of 2007 overtook us. To lay blame for the book's long gestation and change in focus at the door of the 'credit crunch' would be only half true – our underestimation of the task ahead of us was our fault alone. Nevertheless, we are indebted to many individuals and organisations for their assistance and cajoling, without which the book would have remained an unfinished undertaking. Peter Malpass, Peter Williams and Andy Tice provided some invaluable pointers on an early draft. Alan Dearling and Jeremy Spencer were assiduous and thorough in their efforts to turn our manuscript into the finished product. The book is enlivened by the inclusion of photographs and cuttings which appear courtesy of others. Janis Bright helped us source the *Housing Today* article on page 71, which she wrote in 2001. The Stoke *Sentinel* and *Daily Express* have both kindly consented to us reproducing various articles, and Paul Keenan gave us permission to reproduce his map of Newcastle's west end. Carolyn Fox provided us with invaluable assistance in preparing the manuscript and sourcing original materials and rights for reproduction. Finally, as commissioning editor John Perry displayed unending patience and his initial discussions with Alan Murie gave rise to the idea for the book, and we are grateful to them both for the opportunity to take the idea forward. Final thanks go to Ali and Fumie who were unswerving in their support and tolerance of us throughout. The maps and analyses in this volume contain Ordnance Survey data © Crown copyright and database right. Census output is Crown copyright and is reproduced with the permission of the Controller of HMSO and the Queen's Printer for Scotland.

The Chartered Institute of Housing would like to thank Places for People for sponsoring the production of this book. Their work in Walker Riverside (in the Bridging NewcastleGateshead Pathfinder) is reflected in the cover photographs.

CHAPTER 1:
The context for sustainable housing markets: social exclusion and 'rescaling'

Introduction

This book is concerned with what happens when the market for housing in particular areas becomes so problematic that we need to think of ways of intervening. It is partly about those processes of low and changing demand for housing that were so painfully evident towards the end of the 1990s, and the policy developments like Housing Market Renewal (HMR) that emerged as a result. But it is also about a wider set of questions: how can housing markets be kept 'in step' with the society and economy that surrounds them? What happens when gaps appear? How can we rebuild housing markets so that they work better for society and are more in tune with the economy? These questions tax us during good times and bad. At the height of the low-demand problem the national press regularly ran features on the 'hopelessness' of northern estates; and no one surely can forget tales of abandonment, of houses being sold for pittances and of 'spirals of decline'. Less than half a decade later, house prices in many of the same places seemed to have risen so much that the lack of affordable housing in even the most marginal of neighbourhoods became the predominant concern.

The credit crunch and changing demand

Whilst we were writing and researching for this book the world entered into an unprecedented period of economic decline and falls in house prices associated with the 'credit crunch' and the collapse of the sub-prime housing market. This book concentrates on the problems of, and response to, low and changing demand for housing. This is a topic that we have been close to and, along with colleagues in both CURS and at the University of Sheffield, have written about, and contributed to, over the past decade. Whilst we remained cautious about the real benefits of inexorable rises in house prices resulting largely from deregulation and the availability of cheap credit, we could not have anticipated the scale of the downturn and how the housing market would be so inextricably implicated in the large-scale disruption to people's lives. Therefore, whilst not specifically about the credit crunch, this book is wholly concerned with learning the lessons from the low and changing demand phenomenon: the analysis, policy prescription, and implementation of Housing Market Renewal (HMR); and how we might act with purpose to secure sustainable housing markets in a post-credit crunch environment.

Before going any further at this point, it is worth setting out that the housing market has shown signs of failure in a wide variety of contexts. While we inevitably focus in this book on the 'bottom end' of the market, there have been (and are) clear examples of what goes wrong when housing and planning policy fails to detect or foresee mismatches between supply and demand at the higher end of the market too. Indeed, recent events have crystallised this issue somewhat. It has become evident that much of the growth in the market has been in some senses artificial – and this has in turn backed a model for 'sweating assets' in the public sector as well as providing exploitable development value to fund affordable housing (Crook *et al.*, 2006). Growth has occurred in response to a set of demands that has become ever more disassociated from the concept of 'need' for housing as 'shelter'. Such 'excess' demand has underpinned affordability problems that are, in effect, themselves outcomes of market failure. Thus, although we concentrate in this book on local markets that fail at the 'bottom end', much of the principles about understanding how changes in demand occur and why, apply equally to 'higher end' housing markets.

By writing through the 'lens' of low and changing demand we highlight the universal problem associated with markets and the continual need to monitor the relationship between housing and labour markets at a variety of spatial scales. The low and changing demand debate and the credit crunch are part of the same storyline – one of asymmetries between markets (housing, financial, labour) which ultimately result in the need for intervention by the state. The argument is about the type of intervention, its sequencing and scale and the mechanisms of implementation.

Looking back to the turn of this century, it was clear that the most severe manifestation of the low and changing demand phenomenon occurred in the North and Midlands of England (and other parts of the UK such as South Wales and Central Scotland) where there was evidence of high levels of abandonment. Whilst the evidence of abandonment was the most alarming and distressing sign of 'failure', it is still difficult to determine what this was truly a failure of. The causes of changing housing demand, as we discuss in Chapter 2, are varied and occur at a variety of spatial scales. In the various critiques of the policy of HMR that we pick up on later in the book, local authorities themselves were often held to be responsible for market failure by designating Compulsory Purchase Orders (CPOs) and boarding up and neglecting properties and neighbourhoods, long before the HMR programme was announced (Figure 1.1). However, these 'bureaucratic' accounts, which identify local authorities as the main instrument contributing to market failure, are contrasted by more structural explanations. From this perspective, abandoned properties were but a spatial manifestation of a change in the nature of demand that resulted from deindustrialisation and the collapse of Fordist methods of production and consumption in the economy.

Figure 1.1: Boarded up terrace housing in Handsworth, Birmingham, 2003

Source: CURS, University of Birmingham.

Some key junctures can be discerned, such as the post-war planning era and decentralisation of planning in the conurbations (1945-51), the post-IMF crisis (1975), the first government under Margaret Thatcher (1979) and, subsequently, the deregulation of financial markets during the 1980s and 1990s. All of these macro-level structural factors applied nationally. However, the form and style of residential developments throughout urban Britain are uneven and this spatial unevenness, coupled with the uneven temporal effects of policy, has meant that problems manifested themselves differently throughout the country.

As a consequence, local context and micro-level factors also became important in determining whether one place and not another experienced abandonment. One of the most frustrating aspects of the debate surrounding Housing Market Renewal has been the naivety of the journalistic reporting, which periodically surfaced to make the absurd comparison of terrace properties in a deprived northern town or city, with the fortunes (usually measured in house price terms) of a similar property in the south of England (more usually in gentrified districts of London) (see, for example, *Tonight with Trevor McDonald*, 16 May 2005, and Save Britain's Heritage, 2006). Such comparisons are clearly problematic, although they do serve to point out the asymmetry between macro and micro-level factors, and how the 'path dependency' of spaces and their development has contributed to diverging housing market trajectories. In Chapter 2 we look at the case of Liverpool, exploring the micro and macro-level factors in some more depth to consider the underlying causes of abandonment, low demand for housing and neighbourhood change.

By looking at the relationship between the micro and macro-levels, therefore, the subject of this book is again inextricably bound with that of the crisis promulgated by the credit crunch from autumn 2007 onwards, the ramifications of which will remain for some time to come. It is about the continual asymmetry between markets and people, and how they behave. The low and changing demand phenomenon and the credit crunch reflect two separate but related market failures, both of which have required intervention of one form or another. The lesson, clearly, is that market conditions change. Demand changes, neighbourhoods change and new houses are built – sometimes in those same neighbourhoods, sometimes elsewhere. Just as the current economic downturn has its roots in the (institutional) collapse of the housing market, so the changes go on; and questions about the viability of neighbourhoods and of the fit between the housing market and the economy and society's needs seem as pertinent as ever.

Turning to its treatment of the policy response of Housing Market Renewal, this book is therefore about an attempt on the part of a range of actors to 'do something about' the housing market at the turn of the 20th century. Housing Market Renewal broke with the tradition of regeneration initiatives by focusing much more specifically on the market (and its outcomes) than on housing conditions *per se*. The programme has not been without its critics. But we believe that sufficient time has now passed that we can begin to learn lessons from the experience of HMR: to learn whether and how we can try to directly manipulate local housing markets as an instrument of urban policy. The need to understand this is as urgent as ever as we grapple with a new housing future in uncertain times.

Frameworks for understanding market interventions

In tackling the subject of 'building sustainable housing markets' we have set ourselves a difficult task, as this is a broad topic which requires engagement with a wide range of disciplines of study (demography, economy, sociology), and policy areas (planning and urban policy, social policy, housing policy and urban design), to both understand the underlying causes, and design the necessary tools to tackle it. To tackle such a project inevitably requires some parameters in order to structure and frame the analysis and to give the reader a sense of perspective. Without such a framework we will struggle to make sense of both the analysis and the responses to changing and low demand and to rebuild housing markets in a sustainable fashion.

In this first chapter we attempt to define our perspective. We see the low-demand discourse of the late 1990s and early 2000s, and the subsequent policy prescription of HMR, as being largely dependent on a 'rescaled' analysis of space on the one hand and, on the other, an inherent focus on the role of 'place' in reproducing social exclusion. What do we mean by this?

Simply put, the state's concern shifted from housing as an inherently local problem to housing as a sub-regional asset within the wider economy while, at the local level, we began to understand housing not only as a physical problem, but as linked to place – towns and neighbourhoods – which could determine access to wider social opportunities. To focus on the housing market means adopting a perspective on housing that sees it quite clearly as part of a wider social and spatial system.

As we argue in this chapter, there were two underlying reasons for the rising importance of low and changing demand and the concomitant policy response. Firstly, low and changing demand for housing was seen as a spatial reflection of processes of social exclusion. Tackling low and changing demand was bound up with a concern to deliver social and economic inclusion across the regions of England. New Labour's commitment to tackling social exclusion, which was its overarching policy goal in its first term, was therefore an important determinant of both analysis and policy in this area. Secondly, there was a significant change in the analytical framework for housing and its linkage with other policy areas, best understood as a process of 'rescaling' (Collinge, 1999; Uitermark, 2002). Rescaling arguments meant that the 'local' manifestations of changing and low demand for housing began to be interpreted within a larger, more cross-cutting spatial framework, so that the region became, *'the prime geographical unit in the new round of capital accumulation'* (Uitermark, 2002, p.744). Housing was therefore increasingly framed in the context of the contribution it could make to regional processes of social inclusion and economic growth.

Somerville (2004) observes that contributions to the rescaling debate have asserted that the state became, *'...reorganised geographically, such that various state functions and responsibilities were in effect "rescaled"'* (Somerville, 2004, p.137). In some cases, this has led to the proliferation of local agencies while, in others, more global structures have predominated in a process popularly known (after Swyngedouw, 1992) as 'glocalisation'. It is perhaps, however, the rise of the regional scale that is most pertinent to housing market change and of the most interest to us. This was identifiable in both the analysis of low and changing demand and in the policy responses, which were not seen simply in terms of neighbourhood renewal, but in the wider spatial context of sub-regional economies. Of course, as we note in Chapter 2 there has been a rescaling over time which has preceded HMR. For example, economic policy was developed but largely ignored in the 1970s, which might have served to avoid problems of low demand in the 1990s. What we have seen in general is a rescaling of policy interventions to tackle things at a much broader scale.

As we go on to acknowledge in the following chapter, the process of housing abandonment resulting from 'obsolescence' in the face of economic change was by no means a new phenomenon. This can be adequately demonstrated by reference to the infamous cases of the Durham 'D' Villages, Corby or the Glasgow Gorbals. 'Low demand' for housing had happened before, although we would posit that the circumstances and context were very different. It is therefore appropriate to ask why low and changing demand became such a focal point for housing policy during the 1990s; why the analysis rapidly led to the development of the HMR programme, and why it was deemed so important to tackle the underlying drivers of changing and low demand in such a systematically focused way by intervening directly in the housing market.

As we noted above, low and changing demand is a broad topic which requires engagement with a range of disciplines and policy areas. We could arguably have started our analysis at any number of points in time in explaining and understanding the processes. However, both the social exclusion agenda from the mid to late 1990s onwards and the rescaling arguments are uniquely linked. They relate to changes in the political economy of cities and regions. Low and changing demand was as much a debate that questioned economic policy as it was one that asked questions of housing policy and housing strategy. This allowed the housing problem to be fitted neatly into an emerging perspective on exclusion and the role of housing in recreating patterns of exclusion. The social exclusion agenda and the rescaling process together provide an overarching explanation for the direction of travel and the emphasis of policy development over the past decade; a decade in which the interpretation of housing's role as a contributor to social exclusion moved from a narrow analysis of 'worst estates' and homelessness, as demonstrated by the Social Exclusion Unit's (SEU's) remit in 1997, to a broader thematic and spatial analytical framework. In this sense, there has been a confluence of policy and ideology. Key to this has been New Labour's interpretation of what constitutes social exclusion and the emphasis in Whitehall on 'joined-up thinking' from 1997 onwards.

Social exclusion and New Labour

It is helpful to recall that the concept of social exclusion represented a departure from traditional interpretations of poverty. During the 1990s, linkages between the role of *place* and *space* in determining opportunities and life chances were being emphasised. Traditional responses to entrenched or spatially concentrated poverty were acknowledged to be inadequate. Although this was partly because of a growth in social polarisation, the lack of policy co-ordination resulting from a 'silo' culture was also recognised as a factor reinforcing social exclusion (Room, 1995). Both of these facets challenged a traditional household and individual-level 'poverty' approach (i.e., measuring and tackling low incomes and poor resources at household/individual level). The concept of social exclusion encapsulated a more dynamic process: one embedded in the *experiences* of marginalised households, partly encompassed by accounts of how *place* determines outcomes (for example, see Lee and Murie, 1997; Room, 1995, and more latterly Fitzpatrick, 2005). But, historically, accounts of the role that place plays in poverty had tended to be maligned as belonging to a discredited 'culture of poverty' thesis (Lewis, 1966; Murray, 1990). Even more liberal accounts such as William Julius Wilson's (Wilson,

1990) tended to conflate structural and behavioural accounts in arriving at conclusions which unambiguously pointed to a ghettoised *underclass* responsible for its own poverty.

During the 1990s, New Labour recognised that the political vacuum on poverty required filling. In the 1970s, Townsend (1979) had established a relative poverty line that could be used for the implementation of minimum income levels. Social exclusion was a more malleable concept that could be applied to a myriad of circumstances both at an individual and geographical level and was therefore a politically useful and adaptable tool. The rhetoric of social exclusion was therefore less specific about income thresholds and levels of household benefit than the language of poverty was, and this might partly explain its attractiveness to a new government that was concerned about urban poverty and in search of new policy prescriptions.

The popular consensus remained that poverty and social exclusion were contested – poverty for many was absolute rather than relative and for many others, social exclusion remained (and remains) an awkwardly indefinable concept. But in creating exemplars of what New Labour meant when it defined social exclusion, the concept could be neatly packaged and be subjected to policy treatment. The role of place was crucial in this respect as it defined the problem along populist and spatially discrete lines (e.g. the 'worst council housing estates' (Figure 1.2), homelessness, teenage pregnancy and cultures of poverty), and it appealed to an electorate's innate sense of

Figure 1.2: Tackling social exclusion through housing on 'the worst council housing estates': Castle Vale, Birmingham

Source: CURS, University of Birmingham.

moral righteousness. In August 1997, Peter Mandelson committed the government to tackle problems of social exclusion on the 1,370 'worst estates' in England (Mandelson, 1997). Prior to this, Tony Blair's first public speech as prime minister was given outside one of the 'worst estates' in London, where he committed to include the 'forgotten people of Britain' (SEU, 1998). Both interventions emblematically provided a relative spatial reference point for social exclusion: white working-class council estates, either in the inner city or in peripheral locations, whose original economic functions had been lost.

Levitas (1998) had identified three earlier strands to New Labour thinking on social exclusion. First, she identified an integrationist account broadly comprising exclusion from the world of work. The second strand drew on a traditional poverty approach characteristic of the centre left and the Fabian Society; and, third, there was an underclass account, which identified the socially excluded as the most problematic aspects of, and challenges for, social policy – the by-products of a post-industrial society following almost two decades of monetarism and a neo-liberal economy. Despite these three analyses, in its first term New Labour's articulation of social exclusion drew on entirely narrow populist conceptions. The establishment of the SEU (the government's catalyst for policy on social exclusion) reinforced this perception. School truancies, homelessness and teenage pregnancies were added to the problems to be found within the 'worst estates', which themselves were the areas to be targeted and prioritised. In so doing, New Labour initially aligned itself with a narrow interpretation of the socially excluded as an *underclass*, albeit one with a distinct and narrowly-defined spatiality.

But, New Labour's 'worst estates' were an inherited concept, which demonstrated the degree to which political ideology was absent from these debates and how far the New Labour project had to inhabit centre-right ideas in order to be elected. The previous Conservative administration of John Major had published a housing white paper stating that it would tackle the problems of the most deprived estates over the forthcoming decade by getting the Government Offices for the Regions and local authorities to work together to identify, '...*the best way of tackling the estates with the worst social, economic and housing problems*' (DoE, 1995, p.35). However, New Labour recognised the importance of exclusion from employment and the knock-on effect of being out of work. A narrow populist interpretation of exclusion (an underclass account) was therefore not going to fit with New Labour and the Treasury's support for a liberal employment market alongside its support for the New Deal and a minimum wage. The commissioning by the SEU of several Policy Action Team (PAT) reports on a range of topics reflected the diversity of the government's approach to understanding the causes and consequences of social exclusion. However, the emphasis on Jobs (PAT 1), Skills (PAT 2), Business (PAT 3), Neighbourhood Management (PAT 4), Housing Management (PAT 5), Neighbourhood Wardens (PAT 6) and Unpopular Housing (PAT 7) in the first seven of the 18 reports indicated the degree to which the Social Exclusion Unit saw the relationship between the economy, employment and neighbourhood conditions as the important determinants of social exclusion. The National Strategy for Neighbourhood Renewal (NSNR) emerged out of the SEU and explicitly recognised the link between poverty and low demand for housing (SEU, 2001).

Rescaling the problem

The SEU therefore located the causes of social exclusion within a wider framework, rejecting a narrowly conceived spatial framework for exclusion such as the 'worst estates' and referring to the need for 'joined up solutions' to combat 'joined up problems' (SEU, 1998). This period of policy development represented a fundamental reassessment of the role that housing and place played in social exclusion and the policy implications for tackling spatial manifestations of social exclusion.

The low and changing demand debate therefore emerged in a period when there was a concern for tackling poverty and social exclusion by joining up analyses of the problem and looking at the inter-relationship between different policy areas such as employment, welfare benefits, housing, neighbourhoods and schools. As we show in Chapter 2, the drivers of low and changing demand were identified at a number of spatial scales, cutting across not just housing tenures but also local authority boundaries. The notion of the 'worst estates' was, as an analytic framework, too simplistic and did not explain the causes and drivers of the phenomenon. Moreover, the policy solutions to the 'worst estates' would imply an emphasis on tackling the symptoms and spatial manifestations of those symptoms rather than their causes.

More pertinent to the rescaling of the analysis, this period of policy development presaged a growing interest in cross-boundary and cross-authority analysis which was a catalyst for innovations to the evidence base for policy. In Chapter 4 we show how the functional 'Housing Market Area' as a spatial analytical framework came to be cemented and, henceforth, the need arose for *market driven* information ('market intelligence'), rather than data driven by pre-existing administrative boundaries or dictated by local authority political or service delivery functions.

At the turn of the millennium, the evidence base on social exclusion and deprivation was highly dependent on the government's own Index of Local Conditions (ILC). The National Strategy for Neighbourhood Renewal was informed by such indices which measured the problem in increasingly detailed ways, both spatially and thematically. Whilst the ILC represented an improvement on previous attempts by the department responsible for housing, planning and the environment, it was a 'rear view mirror' measure of spatial disadvantage: i.e., it reflected the outcome of processes rather than an explication of the problems and drivers. In summary, the ILC and its successors (including the Index of Multiple Deprivation) were static measures of deprivation, insensitive to the trajectories of space and place and the problems of changing demand.

There was therefore an emerging need to begin to differentiate the *functions* and *trajectories* of deprived areas, as reflected in the type of housing they contained and in their economic function. This would enable an analysis that could differentiate between:

1. deprived areas that were stable and popular, where the demand for housing was robust and therefore the neighbourhood was functioning effectively; and
2. deprived areas where the housing and labour markets had become so out of step with one another and where the housing and neighbourhood characteristics signalled a high risk of changing demand, exposing them to future problems of potential abandonment and/or high levels of population turnover.

While both types of areas were deprived, it is the second type that would be more likely to represent a drag on the national and regional economy. Furthermore, such areas would also be more susceptible to social problems arising from low levels of 'social cohesion'.

It is interesting that early reports from the national press on low demand and the failure of the housing market began to juxtapose accounts of the exclusion at an individual level against the structural failings of the market (see Figure 1.3). In analytical terms, it was becoming increasingly clear that what was required was a measure of the 'asymmetry' between housing and labour markets, capable of capturing the lag between (relatively) fixed housing assets on the one hand and fluid and flexible flows of capital on the other.

Chapter 3 therefore reflects on the evidence base that informed policy on housing market renewal. The evidence is situated in a framework that acknowledges the spatial scale and location of the problem. The asymmetry of housing and labour markets is partly masked by the role that households and individuals play in making choices, decisions and expressing their aspirations – often trading off long-term and short-term goals. The frameworks informing policy on HMR therefore utilised analysis which identified the dynamics of household decisions and aspirations in the housing market and how this affected changing demand. These frameworks reflected an ongoing preoccupation with social exclusion, differentiating between excluded spaces. But, as Chapter 3 shows, the evidence base was also beginning to articulate a preoccupation with the 'path dependency' of places, and their relationship to (previous) policy eras, where housing was built to support specific economic functions. The analysis began to offer a new way of thinking about housing, which was concerned with the re-alignment of housing and housing markets to support the emerging economy or to proactively influence the kind of economy that could be developed in the future. The implication, of course, is that a 'rescaled' spatial framework for the analysis of the problem needed to be matched by a similarly rescaled policy framework.

Figure 1.3: Early reports from the press on low demand

Source: *The Daily Express*, Friday 25 June 1999.

The Sustainable Communities Plan of 2003, which ushered in HMR, was in some ways a substitute for the national spatial strategy that had been called for by some of the architects of Housing Market Renewal (see for example, Nevin, 2001). The Sustainable Communities Plan offered a set of policy measures to tackle the twin problems of low demand in the North and Midlands on the one hand and affordability pressures in the South on the other. It was redolent of the contested notion of a 'North-South divide' in England, one which the government refused to acknowledge (Hall and Hickman, 2004). It introduced new regional governance structures for housing, in the shape of regional housing boards, which were to parallel regional planning bodies. In these regional housing boards, a stronger regional arena was provided that was to enable a more detailed commentary on regional housing needs than had been hitherto provided for by regional planning guidance. Therefore, although the Sustainable Communities Plan was not a national spatial strategy, it encompassed the most comprehensive official endorsement of the *rescaling* of housing to provide a framework by which housing could be understood and related to the economic strategy for the regions.

The development of more holistic regional spatial strategies (RSSs) reflected this need to make the most effective use of land for housing and to align this with the needs of the economy. To enable this, RSSs have to date utilised an ever more detailed and comprehensive analysis of housing market trends, in order to draw out implications for the location and scale of housing developments at regional and sub-regional level. They have served to maximise the role of housing policy and strategy as a lever of planning policy, aiming to balance demand across wider spaces and influence household mobility through the regionalisation of housing supply decisions. A more detailed understanding of the role of housing markets within the region and the interaction of housing market intelligence with economic and planning drivers has therefore been a facet of the rescaling of housing and its fit within the political economy of regions.

The competitive city and social exclusion

Since the mid 1990s there has been a growing concern for the competitiveness of British cities and a burgeoning evidence base demonstrating how they lag behind their European counterparts in terms of productivity and economic output (ODPM, 2004a). The inefficiencies of the English cities within the 'core cities' grouping (Birmingham, Bristol, Leeds, Liverpool, Manchester, Newcastle upon Tyne, Nottingham and Sheffield) stem from decline in the 1960s, 1970s and 1980s, when the focus was on the problems and challenges posed, as Margaret Thatcher put it, by *'…those inner cities'* (Robson, 1988). During the 1990s, cities once again became fashionable and came to be seen as economic assets rather than liabilities, presaging renewed investment, cultural development and a strengthened appetite for urban lifestyles. This has also been reflected in an increasingly intense competition between cities in a global environment and the predominance of a 'knowledge economy' in the production of both goods and services. The implications of this for planning and housing were crystallised by the findings of Lord Rogers' Urban Task Force (1999). However, whilst the core cities have undergone an economic renaissance over the past decade they still fail to fully punch their weight economically in the national context. Consequently, they have continued to fall behind London and the South East, and *'…do not make as great a contribution to the national economic welfare, as comparable cities* [do] *in continental Europe'* (ODPM, 2004a, p.6). This gave rise to initiatives such as the Northern Way, in which the northern regional development agencies sought and continue to seek synergies across regional boundaries, emphasising the importance of supra-regional infrastructure and local 'quality of life' in bringing about economic development (Northern Way Steering Group, 2004).

However, in some ways the core cities represent anachronistic spatial entities within the modern political economy of regions. The core cities are by and large, ex-industrial, and the re-alignment of their economies towards a new service and knowledge-based economy has meant that they can no longer be seen as autonomous, self-contained spatial units. Rather than simply being cities in their own right, they draw on a wider set of spatial reference points which cut across local authority and regional boundaries, making them increasingly dependent on a broader (and more spatially dispersed) pool of labour with a variety of skills to service the needs of these emerging service and knowledge economies.

The demise of the local authority as a reference point for the local economy was symbolised by Thatcherism's incessant assault on local councils and the creation of urban development corporations in the 1980s, which by-passed elements of local authority control (Thomas and Imrie, 1997). The creation of regional development agencies in 1998 was a distinctive moment in the rescaling story but, importantly for our account, one that failed to sufficiently acknowledge either the role of housing or the housing market in these spatial alignments (Robinson, 2003). Making good this deficit can be seen to be one of the intentions behind the creation of the nine Housing Market Renewal Pathfinders in 2003 (see the map in Appendix 1). However, from the beginning of the millennium there was an emerging argument for a new set of functional entities by which services were to be delivered to meet the needs of a modernised economy. This has resulted in the importance of city regions, 'functional entities' that have been increasingly acknowledged and supported by central government (ODPM, 2006). The role of city regions in building urban and regional competitiveness and reducing regional imbalance is perhaps the most recent example of the rescaling of housing and its role within the political economy, both nationally and at the regional and sub-regional level. It introduces a more embedded set of analyses, conjoining the economy and the role of housing and the neighbourhood. But it has a clear economic agenda: whilst the competitiveness of cities is dependent on a set of relationships beyond the core city boundary, housing is but one of a series of factors that are viewed as essential to the delivery of the competitive service and knowledge-based economy:

> Our rationale for working together as a city region partnership is simple. Global investors and decision makers do not recognise local authority boundaries. Their interest is in understanding the local economy as a whole – a cluster of mutually interdependent areas linked economically and socially by travel to work patterns, by housing, retail and leisure markets, and by population needs and skills. They want to know whether this local economy possesses the infrastructure and assets that global businesses need in order to establish themselves and grow (Our City Region, 2005, para. 7).

These developments in the arguments for city regions and the competitiveness of cities, force the analysis of, and response to, housing market problems into closer alignment with those arguments that emphasise the need for modernisation of the (sub) regional economy. This implies that the way in which HMR can assist in that process is by funding the re-modelling of markets in order to attract different household types or demand cohorts. In order to be competitive, the thinking goes, city regions need to attract and retain the right kind of workforce for a knowledge-based/creative economy to prosper. By rescaling the analytical framework to take account of the sub-regional and regional economy and the housing market's function within this, housing and neighbourhoods come to be seen to be located within a much broader spatial framework. This has created the opportunity to develop a narrative around housing market renewal as an adjunct to economic development policy and planning at the regional level. Although the low-demand debate of the late 1990s and the creation of HMR was aimed at redressing an imbalance in the market and the relationship between housing and the economy, the analysis lent itself to a much wider spatial context than that covered even by the HMR Pathfinders. This resulted eventually in the more ambitious Northern Way and city region development plans (CRDPs) subsuming the HMR principle within a broader and grander strategy for extracting greater performance from regional economies.

Foresight and resilience

The new system of development plans brought in under the Planning and Compulsory Purchase Act 2004 strengthened the spatial scalar framework in which analyses of housing demand and plans for meeting it are articulated. The publication of Planning Policy Statement 3 (PPS 3) on Housing (CLG, 2006a) re-emphasised the importance and relevance of housing market information for regional planning bodies and local planning authorities when developing planning policies. Market information on housing is cascaded down the planning system (i.e., regional spatial strategies through to Local Development Frameworks or LDFs) informed by an evidence base of housing need and demand and delivered through Strategic Housing Market Assessments (SHMAs).

In determining the local, sub-regional and regional level of housing provision, local planning authorities and regional planning bodies are asked to take into account evidence on future need and demand for housing, affordability levels and '...*the needs of the regional economy, having regard to economic growth forecasts*' (CLG, 2006a, p.12). The 'credit crunch' has demonstrated the tenuous nature of links between our economic and housing market intelligence and the fragility of assumptions that are overly dependent on the extrapolation of linear trends. As we later speculate in Chapter 6, there will be an increasing need to develop interactive models of demand and supply which integrate different economic scenarios and their housing implications. Beyond this, the economics of environmental sustainability will demand that sustainability parameters will need to be developed and be part of the housing market assessment evidence base if successive governments are to deliver on their commitments to reduce carbon emissions. Housing policy and creating efficiencies in the spatial alignment of housing with economic needs can deliver effectively on this agenda as PPS 1 on *Delivering Sustainable Development* recognises (ODPM, 2005c; see also RTPI and CLG, 2008).

Therefore, the governance and policy development arrangements for planning and housing have increasingly reflected processes of rescaling embodied in the analytical framework for low and changing demand. Assets contained within neighbourhoods and local housing markets are more often being called upon to deliver wider regional strategies. The ongoing convergence of regional housing, spatial and economic strategies into a single regional strategy reflects institutional attempts to rescale the role of housing and calibrate it with economic and planning drivers for growth.

Building sustainable housing markets

Whilst this book is not ostensibly about New Labour housing policy, it does use the period of its government since 1997 as a timeframe for understanding the underlying political motivations behind the policy responses to changing and low demand as well as efforts to tackle social exclusion. As we have noted above, the low and changing demand debate arose in a period when tackling social exclusion was a central part of the government's thinking. In Housing Market Renewal, the response to low demand was quickly absorbed into a set of agendas around the competitive city, the needs of a creative and knowledge-based economy and governance arrangements for city regions resulting from the rescaling of the analytical framework for housing.

However, the emphasis on competitiveness and the underpinning needs of a service and knowledge-based economy, within a broader set of spatial linkages, has effectively resulted in a competition to attract new, higher-income earners to low-demand areas. This has inevitably elicited arguments that an imbalanced focus on middle-class groups may have contributed to a blind-spot in processes of community consultation or concern for the views of existing (largely working-class) residents (Allen, 2008). Thinking back to the framework we propose in this book, it could be argued that the result has been a backgrounding of social exclusion as a policy concern within the delivery of Housing Market Renewal and an emphasis, instead, on modernisation or *de facto* state sponsored gentrification, charges which are promoted by critics like Allen (2008) and Cameron (2006).

Yet we contend in this book that building and delivering sustainable housing markets requires an analysis that engages at the appropriate spatial scale (rescaling housing policy, which may involve some form of 'rebalancing' the housing market), and which also accommodates a community perspective (social inclusion and cohesion). This requires balance. If housing is to find a comfortable way of delivering all of the multiple demands placed on it; if it is to continue to perform its function as shelter, while providing a supporting role to a competitive economy, as an investment commodity and as a form of welfare redistribution, then it will need to be increasingly sensitive to the contradictory spatial and functional requirements being placed upon it. This book provides an opportunity to understand how we have begun to articulate sustainability in terms of housing markets, how and why Housing Market Renewal was seen as a model for delivering sustainable housing markets, and what the future prospects are for building sustainable housing markets within the current and foreseeable policy context.

The vicissitudes of the housing market over the period that this has been written has demanded that we title this contribution as *'Building Sustainable Housing Markets'*, as we are concerned with charting the development of HMR as well as understanding its legacy, impact and lessons for dealing with the ongoing challenge of intervening in the housing market in an effective and appropriate way.

Table 1.1 summarises the key events that chart the development of this ambitious and controversial programme.

Table 1.1: Key publications and events

Date	Event
July 1998	Conference on *Housing Abandonment in the English Inner City* held at York University bringing together new research on 'low demand' for housing. See Lowe *et al.* (1998).
1999	Joseph Rowntree Foundation report into the *Slow Death of Great Cities* looks at the multifaceted nature of neighbourhood decline in Newcastle and Manchester. See Power and Mumford (1999).
1999	Policy Action Team (PAT) report 7 on *Unpopular Housing* reported on low demand, highlighting significant levels in social rented housing stock alongside a prevalence in the private sector, especially in the North West region.
January 2000	Summary of Housing Corporation-sponsored report (Cole *et al.*, 1999) into housing association responses to low demand is published. The report garners significant media attention, mainly centred on the report's claims that demolition and 'managing decline' may be inevitable in some neighbourhoods. *The Independent* runs a prominent article entitled, *'Northern estates "are beyond any salvation"'* (6 January 2000).
February 2001	CURS 'M62 Corridor' study (Nevin, Lee *et al.*, 2000) published. The report was commissioned by a consortium of local authorities and housing associations concerned with increasing vacancies and high turnover of low-income housing stock. →

THE CONTEXT FOR SUSTAINABLE HOUSING MARKETS

Date	Event
June 2001	Department of the Environment, Transport and the Regions (DETR) scrapped and replaced by Department for Transport, Local Government and Regions (DTLR). Stephen Byers MP heads the department.
March 2002	A select committee report into *Empty Homes* (HC 240-I, 2001-02) looks into the issue of abandonment and housing market failure in the North and Midlands of England. Using emotive examples, it calls for urgent action and the establishment of a market renewal fund.
April 2002	DTLR announces the creation of nine HMR Pathfinders with 'seedcorn' funding from the Capital Modernisation Fund.
May 2002	Office of the Deputy Prime Minister (ODPM) is established and absorbs the DTLR portfolio. ODPM is headed by John Prescott MP.
February 2003	The 'Sustainable Communities Plan' (ODPM, 2003) establishes the £500 million Housing Market Renewal Fund (HMRF) for the three years 2003/04 to 2005/06.
July 2004	Treasury spending review allocates a further £450 million to the HMRF for the two years 2006/07 to 2007/08.
December 2004	Cole and Nevin (2004) publish *The Road to Renewal*, the first major account of the development of HMR.
January 2005	ODPM publishes its *Homes For All* five year plan (ODPM, 2005a), which sets out specific objectives for the HMR programme. The plan also announces further funding (to take the total value of the HMRF since inception to £1.2 billion) and recognises three additional HMR areas in Teesside, West Cumbria and West Yorkshire, which will share a top-sliced £65 million budget.
April 2005	House of Commons select committee enquiry into *Empty Homes and Low Demand Pathfinders* reports (HC 295-I, 2004-05). The committee was concerned that government did not have clear objectives for what HMR was trying to achieve.
May 2005	*Beatles* drummer Ringo Starr, whose birthplace home becomes earmarked for demolition by Liverpool City Council, speaks out against the HMR programme.
June 2005	An edition of the television magazine programme *Tonight with Trevor McDonald* focuses on HMR and raises questions about its necessity. At around the same time, *The Daily Telegraph's* environment correspondent Charles Clover writes a series of scathing articles about HMR, with criticism mainly directed at John Prescott. →

Date	Event
January 2006	The Home Office launches its Respect Action Plan as part of a strategy to reduce anti-social behaviour.
April 2006	The three additional HMR partnerships in Teesside, West Cumbria and West Yorkshire are able to access HMRF monies distributed through regional housing boards.
May 2006	Department for Communities and Local Government (CLG) formed, with Ruth Kelly MP as secretary of state.
June 2006	Pathfinders are requested by the housing minister to consider how their plans will help to deliver the Respect Agenda. Later, in October 2006, HMR Pathfinders become clearly involved in its delivery in their areas through the HMR 'Respect Protocol' (CLG, 2006b).
March 2007	An independent evaluation of HMR (Leather *et al.*, 2007) finds that Pathfinders have made considerable progress, but that it is not clear to what extent price rises and other indicators can be directly attributed to HMR investment.
September 2007	An investor 'bank run' on Northern Rock signals the first major UK financial institution to suffer the fallout of the 'credit crunch'. Northern Rock and other similar institutions had highly-leveraged portfolios securitised by properties in lower-priced neighbourhoods.
November 2007	The National Audit Office produces an assessment of the value-for-money of the HMR programme (NAO, 2007). The report is somewhat lukewarm in its endorsement of the HMR approach and makes a number of recommendations aimed at streamlining the delivery of the programme and reducing its impact on communities.
February 2008	CLG minister Iain Wright MP announces a continuation of the HMRF for the three years 2008/09 to 2010/11, with a total budget of just over £1 billion.
April 2008	Tees Valley Living is accorded full HMR 'Pathfinder' status by CLG.
December 2008	The Homes and Communities Agency (HCA) is formed under provisions made in the Housing and Regeneration Act 2008, taking on responsibilities and assets from English Partnerships and the Housing Corporation. The HCA also takes on responsibility for HMR.
May 2009	An Audit Commission programme review report (Audit Commission, 2009) is broadly supportive of the HMR programme and approach, stating that *'the rationale of the HMR programme remains entirely valid'*.

Summary

This book is concerned with what happens when the market for housing in particular areas becomes so problematic that we need to think of ways of intervening. By writing through the 'lens' of low and changing demand for housing we highlight the universal problem associated with markets and the continual need for monitoring the relationship between housing and labour markets at a variety of spatial scales. Therefore, in this sense, the subject of this book is inextricably bound with that of the crisis promulgated by the credit crunch that arose from autumn 2007 onwards, and the ramifications of which will remain for some time to come.

The low and changing demand debate shifted the focus away from core concerns of social exclusion and the household to housing's wider role as a contributor to regional economic competitiveness and this represents a significant rescaling of the role and emphasis of housing policy. Rescaling promulgated significant efforts to reconcile the strategic role of housing and the social exclusion agenda with the desire for greater policy co-ordination to eradicate a 'silo' culture. This was a precursor to the rescaling and competitiveness agenda and housing's role within these debates. The social exclusion narrative also stimulated a wider debate on the role that place plays in contributing to exclusion – the low and changing demand debate highlighted the significant role of place in contributing to abandonment and high turnover which in turn contributed to severe exclusion. The setting up of the Social Exclusion Unit signalled a significant departure away from a 'worst estates' approach – for instance, treating the symptoms and not the causes, to a more systematic and integrated evidence base for understanding social exclusion.

The changing demand debate introduced the idea that there was a need to differentiate between the function and trajectories of deprived areas – deprived areas could be stable and cohesive, whilst low and changing demand areas were qualitatively different types of deprived places. The concept of trajectories and evidence of core cities lagging behind European counterparts provided fertile ground for the emergence of the city-region as a mechanism for reconciling territorial and thematic conflicts and delivering efficiency and growth of gross value added (GVA). Housing markets were a significant part of this narrative. The growing importance of the strategic function of local authorities and agencies reflected in both the shift towards an economic development/competitiveness led planning system (post-Barker) and the introduction of Strategic Housing Market Assessments. The credit crunch and failure of the evidence base indicates the need for a review of forecasting methods and introduction of more holistic foresight/scenario building methods that can reconcile different views of 'reality'.

Structure of the book

Chapter 2 charts the origins of the 'low demand' and 'changing demand' debates, and tracks how deep fissures in the national distribution of housing market performance were leading to tensions between different policies – notably the question of how population change would impact on the need for housing. The structures of the housing market and its relationship to the economy are brought to the fore, supplanting more traditional concerns with the popularity of particular estates or house types. The emergence of the 'region' as a more appropriate geographic unit of analysis and policy response is described. The emerging 'asymmetry' between regional housing and labour markets is advanced as a way of better understanding the direction that future housing and regeneration policy needs to take.

Chapter 3 begins to focus on the evidence that was assembled to support the need for an analysis of housing markets that was more nuanced, geographically astute, and which recognised the multiple links with other policy areas. This multi-dimensionality is highlighted with reference to varied symptoms and causes of changed demand for housing, including the links with local economies, deprivation, and the urban form. A method of assessing the 'risk' of areas suffering from housing demand problems is described and is extended to cover the North and Midlands of England in a consistent analysis. This is set alongside the development of detailed local studies in a number of metropolitan areas, all with the aim of essentially building the case for a concerted long-term approach to tackling housing market weakness.

Chapter 4 is concerned with the ways that the regional and local evidence bases described in Chapter 3 were assembled and deployed as part of a political coalition building exercise aimed at lobbying government for a market renewal fund. The local and regional nature of the analysis and the problem was emphasised, leading to a programme with considerable flexibilities. The process of the nine original HMR Pathfinders developing their strategic thinking and investment plans is described, with particular focus on the range of issues they covered in their 'prospectuses'.

Chapter 5 takes stock of the development of the HMR programme. The chapter considers the activities that the HMR Pathfinders have undertaken to date, and specifically examines their change of strategy away from a focus on demolition. The way that the HMR programme has had to change in response to shifting political priorities and new conceptualisations of the housing problem is considered – in particular, the imperative for Pathfinders to reinvent themselves as agencies of housing growth exemplifies a shift away from the concerns with social exclusion that characterised early New Labour regeneration policy. The nature and impact of a growing body of criticism directed towards Pathfinders and the HMR approach is also considered. The chapter concludes by examining some of the key issues involved in evaluating a complex programme such as HMR and focuses in particular on whether the question of (geographic) scale has been appropriately addressed.

Finally, Chapter 6 attempts to both look back and look forward, summing up a policy and programme that has traversed a diverse range of government priorities and in so doing has embodied a range of objectives. What the lessons of the HMR experience tell us about the possibilities of securing sustainable and resilient housing markets, particularly at the local and regional levels, are a key concern of this final chapter. We conclude that there are real lessons for a range of policy design issues: setting objectives, monitoring and evaluating, strategic planning and an emerging 'place making' agenda.

CHAPTER 2:
The origins: low and changing demand for housing

Introduction

This chapter considers the emergence of the low-demand debate and some of the key literature and evidence that contributed to it in the late 1990s. As we saw in Chapter 1, the Housing Market Renewal policy response partly represented a New Labour concern with social exclusion within neighbourhoods in northern cities that were suffering the fallout from a period of intense economic change. But, it also reflected an increasing desire to rescale the spatial focus of policy; to bring housing much more clearly into the purview of regional economic development imperatives. As the main purpose of this book is to consider the future of sustainable housing markets by providing an account of the policy cycle leading to Housing Market Renewal and beyond, we must begin by revisiting the factors that were seen to be contributing to changing demand for housing over the last decade or so.

By the end of the 20th century, housing policy in the UK had come to embody an explicit recognition of the structural differences in the market between areas of high and low demand. Despite occasional claims to the contrary, the clearest geographical expression of structural market variation – in England and Wales at least – was along a North-South axis (Murie *et al.*, 1998). The emergence of 'low demand' as a housing policy concern was first signalled by the detection of various processes that clearly challenged conventional housing management wisdom. Most important of these was the growing inability of social housing landlords to find tenants for even modern and well-maintained properties, including (notoriously) some brand new developments. There was, on the cusp of the new century, an intense media interest in academic work that suggested that housing problems in northern cities could not be tackled on an *ad hoc*, microscopic basis, but required a strategic approach (Cole *et al.*, 1999). At the philosophical level, the question of whether northern cities had a future was being asked. On 6 January 2000, *The Guardian* reported rather dramatically that Cole *et al.'s* (1999) work suggested that the *'North's sink estates are "beyond saving"'*. *The Independent* ran a similar story on the same day. Some social housing landlords reported that in effect they no longer had a waiting list for general needs housing. Rather than looking to traditional causal factors, such as stock condition, size, or type, attention turned necessarily to structural factors for explanation. Holmans and Simpson (1999) highlighted the role of inter-regional differentiation in migration and the uneven impacts of international immigration as one of the principal structural factors explaining divergent housing market conditions at the regional level. These were quite different from the micro-management concerns of dealing with 'difficult-to-let' stock. The impact of wider structural processes, including the land use planning system, regional economies and labour markets, in giving rise to low-demand conditions was pulled immediately into focus. Low-demand conditions appeared pervasive throughout areas of private sector housing as well as social housing estates (Bramley *et al.*, 2000), fuelling the suspicion that something operating at a different scale was afoot, and that simply improving management or marketing would do little in the long run to improve demand.

Paralleling this, the New Labour government of 1997 had set in train an explicit *neighbourhoods* agenda, which aimed to narrow social exclusion and bring about sustainable regeneration of areas through a holistic concern with a multitude of neighbourhood factors and service areas, including education, transport, employment, health, and crime. The work of the Social Exclusion Unit – at the time directly answerable to the Cabinet Office – and the establishment of the Neighbourhood Renewal Fund constituted the main government policy response. This also built on an emerging design quality and 'liveability' agenda following the convening of the Urban Task Force (1999) and Lord Rogers' exhortations to bring about an 'urban renaissance' in England and Wales (the subsequent urban white paper introduced the 60 per cent brownfield housing target that would form the backbone for planning policy in the 2000s).

Much of the evidence on low and changing demand at the time emphasised spatial and tenure differences and the need to consider the housing market as a whole. But it was also instrumental in developing the links with wider urban and regeneration policies. According to the Department for Communities and Local Government, HMR has gone on to be one of the best evidenced regeneration programmes there has been.[1] It is clear that research and market intelligence played a critical role in its evolution. This chapter begins by briefly reviewing the two related concepts that were writ large across the housing policy debate in the late 1990s: 'low demand' and 'changing demand' for housing. Our attention then turns to an examination of the key issues implicated in analyses of low and changing demand. These include, among other things, changes in local and regional economies; demographic changes; the decentralisation of population; planning policy; changes to the subsidy of housing and the operation of the housing market; and continuing shifts in the attitudes, aspirations and expectations of individuals.

Conceptualising the problem

Housing that nobody wants to live in seems like a simple enough problem. The symptoms are often self-evident and largely incontrovertible. Yet, it is worth remembering that there was some confusion over what the problem of 'low

---

1   Communities and Local Government press release 2007/0032: *'Research shows life in pathfinder areas is improving'* (1 March 2007).

demand' really was. Certainly, it took some time before the symptoms were officially recognised as constituting something different from the types of 'difficult-to-let' social housing management issues that had been evident in Britain's cities for decades. The big differences seemed to be structural rather than local in nature. For instance, it was becoming apparent that it was not a problem confined only to social housing estates or to housing in poor condition. The regional dimension was becoming better understood: it was plain that problems borne of insufficient demand for housing were more prevalent in the North and the Midlands than they were in the South of the country.

But, what of the causes of empty housing and weak local housing markets? The remainder of this chapter deals with the causes in greater detail. However, it is worth pausing briefly to summarise what were seen as the main causes, because these influenced greatly the thinking behind market intervention. It is also worth considering briefly how these various 'drivers of change' played out at different spatial scales. We do so by referring to the case of Liverpool, a city which would go on to find itself at the centre of the policy response to low demand.

In one of the first reports on changing demand and unpopular housing, Alan Murie, Brendan Nevin and Philip Leather identified a number of key factors for a Housing Corporation report published in 1998 (Murie *et al.*, 1998). They pointed then to the restructuring of the local and regional economy, differential rates of migration and the residualisation of social housing as the main contributory factors; to these could be added a range of other macro and micro-level factors such as: the portability of housing benefits, economic and residential decentralisation, over-estimates of regional population growth, low interest rates, area reputation, lettings policies, anti-social behaviour, quality and condition of the housing stock, and type of dwelling.

The argument, as it proceeded, was that in some areas the regional and local economy had undergone radical change, leaving a legacy of socio-spatial polarisation and inequality which had taken time to work itself through the housing market. Neighbourhoods that were built to service a different economic era were being by-passed by a service class. This resulted in a polarised structure within these neighbourhoods, which were mainly to be found in post-war estates and pre-1919 terraces, as a relatively stable but declining older population was being replaced by a younger, more insecure and more transient population. The symptoms of low demand, including high vacancy and turnover rates, were more concentrated in the housing markets of the North and Midlands where the economy had grown at a slower rate than in the South of England. Whilst there were problems with the popularity of some housing estates in the South, these tended to be more confined and bore a clearer relationship with property type, condition and tenure.

At the same time, problems in the North were also being explained with reference to planning decisions in the 1950s in which slum clearance and new, decentralised settlements undermined the conurbation cores and reinforced a pattern of net outward migration from them. These opportunities were of course facilitated by technological and social changes – particularly the proliferation of cheap personal motorised transport. The resulting migration patterns were a result of higher-income groups (although by no means only the wealthy) moving out of conurbations and relocating to expanding market towns and rural locations, leaving behind a skewed population structure. The impact on neighbourhoods had particular tenure dynamics.

Privatisation policies in the 1970s, and especially the right to buy since 1979, had created competition for low-income households renting in the public and private sectors (Jones and Murie, 2006). The supply of public housing had peaked and was by then in decline, while new building in the private sector largely failed to compensate for this. The 'residualisation' of council housing led to a gap in the profile of social rented housing, with mainly the lower paid and older households moving into or remaining in the sector, coupled with the decline of middle-income groups as a result of financial deregulation and privatisation policies (Burrows, 1999). Meanwhile, the portability of benefits and the competition for low-income households meant the private landlord could offer incentives to swap tenures. This created an environment in which landlords competed for a declining market, producing inefficiencies in the management of public housing, and a fragmented public policy framework.

Changing demand in Liverpool

Most of the processes just described occurred to some extent in Liverpool. CURS worked on a number of reports for Liverpool City Council during the period 1998-2003, exploring the low and changing demand phenomenon, its underlying causes and how it affected the city (see for example Groves *et al.*, 2001; Lee and Nevin, 2002; Nevin and Lee, 2003; Nevin *et al.*, 1999). It is easy to forget the scale of abandonment and the feeling of desolation that existed in many neighbourhoods like Granby, captured in the photos in Figures 2.1 and 2.2.

The Liverpool case study highlights the way in which different causal factors came together over different time periods and across space to weaken the local housing market. Looking at some of these in more detail:

- **Diversification of the economy:** during the 1970s and 1980s, Liverpool had a high dependence on manufacturing and relatively low-skilled employment within industries related to shipping and automotive manufacturing. This gave rise to a tight relationship between housing and the local economy. The failure of the city to diversify its economic base alongside housing market interventions would come to have repercussions for changing demand for housing in future waves of economic development (Harding *et al.*, 2004).

- **Decentralisation:** during the 1950s and 1960s, the city experienced a decentralisation of population through the creation of new towns such as Runcorn and Skelmersdale, and the growth of housing in the Wirral. This provision of new housing opportunities encouraged the migration of households out of the city.
- **Expansion of higher education:** the expansion of higher education during this period created the first generation exposed to mass higher education and opportunities to move out of the city and who could subsequently develop careers outside the city. The failure to diversify the economy or the housing market offer in the city, compounded future problems of low and changing demand by failing to create the opportunities or neighbourhood choices for potential returners. At the same time, during the period of expansion, parts of the housing market became revitalised through the housing of students in inner city terrace housing areas. However, the subsequent delivery of bespoke student housing by local universities and the private sector served to further weaken fragile markets by reducing demand for such 'studentified' inner city properties.
- **'Concealed' effects:** household responses to economic restructuring during the 1970s and 1980s often involved the use of occupational pensions and redundancy payments to invest in housing. For these reasons the housing impacts of economic decline were not simultaneous; rather, problems related to housing disinvestment and housing market weakness were concealed at first, and only later began to surface in the mid to late 1990s. Council tax records in the late 1990s recorded a high proportion of payees as being executors of wills: these related to vacant housing resulting from the death of a sole surviving household member.

Figure 2.1: Boarded up shops and housing in Granby, Liverpool, 1999

Source: authors' own.

Figure 2.2: Boarded up private sector housing in Granby, Liverpool, 1999

Source: authors' own.

- **Fragmented governance:** the political instability of the early 1980s, signalled by fractures in the local Labour party and embodied in the influence of the 'Militant tendency', reflected a dissonance between local politics and the structure of economic capital and national economic policy. The city council, then led by Derek Hatton, pursued a policy of investment in additional social housing provision to capture the 'traditional working-class' vote. In the context of economic change, this compounded the problem of over-supply and created further instability in the market. There was a failure to provide an integrated social housing strategy as housing associations operating in the inner city had adopted differential speeds of investment and disinvestment. Private landlords had begun to add to this fragmented structure by taking advantage of right to buy properties and prices kept low in a climate of over-supply.

The overall impact of each of these factors was to create and sustain a vicious circle of decline, cumulatively disadvantaging existing residents and locking them into processes of social exclusion. The failure, in effect, for housing management and strategy at the local level to accommodate an increasing set of external pressures contributed to a highly volatile housing market. Looking back, it is clear that to reconcile local needs with national and global economic pressures required a level of sub-regional planning and a capacity to interpret sub-regional housing market dynamics that did not exist.

Changing demand

Although the symptoms of housing market problems, such as those in Liverpool revealed the extent of demand problems, policy-makers were naturally and rightly also concerned with finding solutions to the problem. This required not only an appreciation of its causes, but a better conceptualisation of the problem. Was it really an issue of 'low demand'? Or was it, as others like Murie *et al.* (1998) argued, something more subtle: the product of changes in demand that, for one reason or another, the market was unable to adjust to and resulted in uneven patterns of demand and supply?

It was this recognition of the complex interplay of forces – at a variety of spatial levels – that led many academics and policy-makers to adopt the term 'changing demand'. Implicit in this was the view that it was rapidly changing local markets that were leading to the worst problems and the inability of policy to keep pace. Furthermore, the concept of 'changing demand' seemed particularly useful in explaining why severe shortfalls in demand were affecting the private sector as much as the social rented sector.

With this in mind, there was considerable interest in trying to gauge the extent to which housing market change was a problem in England. The concern was naturally with those local housing markets that could be identified as 'failing' in some way or another. The changing demand debate made it necessary to try to look beyond housing itself for a way into the problem of quantification. Most researchers adopted a framework – very much in keeping with the 'joined-up' ethos of the time – that attempted to integrate a concern with housing together with wider risk factors in society and neighbourhoods.

Quantifying the problem

Two sets of studies in particular, made significant headway into the problem of quantifying the effects of the low/changing demand phenomenon. The first of these contributions was a national survey of local authorities commissioned by the Social Exclusion Unit and undertaken by a team at Heriot-Watt University led by Glen Bramley (Bramley *et al.*, 2000). This project was the first attempt to provide a consistent national picture of low demand. The authors reported that some 61 per cent of local authorities in England were experiencing low-demand problems and that, together, local authorities in the North East and North West accounted for some 48 per cent of the national problem. The team estimated that a total of 928,000 dwellings in England were affected by low demand, over half of those being in the private sector. An early analysis of these results provided the evidence for the cross-cutting Policy Action Team report into unpopular housing, PAT 7 (SEU, 2000).

A more prognostic attempt to conceptualise areas as being 'at risk' of low or changing demand was undertaken by a team of researchers at the Centre for Urban and Regional Studies at the University of Birmingham (Nevin, Lee *et al.*, 2000). Commissioned by a broad consortium of housing organisations in the North West, the work became known as the 'M62 study' on account of its focus on Greater Manchester and Merseyside. This study found clear evidence of low and changing demand in housing of all tenures and in mixed tenure neighbourhoods. By deploying a relatively sophisticated spatial analysis at the neighbourhood scale (see Chapter 3), they concluded that around 280,000 households, housing nearly 700,000 people in the study area, could be considered to be in neighbourhoods 'at risk' of changing demand. Further work elsewhere in the northern regions (Leather *et al.*, 2002, 2003; Lee, Hall *et al.*, 2002) was subsequently commissioned and consolidated in a 2004 report to the Northern Way consortium of RDAs that suggested that perhaps 1.5 million dwellings were in areas that suffered some risk of low or changing demand (CURS, 2004). This figure proved contentious, although it was often used out of context. As the authors noted:

> *It is not appropriate to place too much emphasis on the absolute numbers of dwellings identified as being at risk, but rather to use the index* [of risk] *as a broad indicator of local authorities and more specific neighbourhoods where there may be a need for housing market restructuring or other forms of intervention* (CURS, 2004, p.10).

CURS's (2004) national map of the risk of low and changing demand confirmed the extent to which it was a problem that largely affected the deindustrialised conurbations in northern regions. Interestingly, the authors' later work provided independent corroboration of Bramley et al.'s (2000) earlier calculations that just under a half of the national low-demand problem was accounted for by the North West and North East. Leather et al. (2007) found that around 42 per cent of national risk was found in those two regions.

One of the clearest findings of researchers working in the field was that low demand somewhat paradoxically coexisted with an overall national picture of additional housing need and, in some other places, the inability for lower-income households to access the housing market. While low demand affected a large number of local authorities across broad contiguous areas it was essentially a problem whose most significant symptoms were localised. The geographic scales at which low demand was operating were confusing – consequently, scale became a very important part of attempts to understand how severe the low-demand problem was.

The location of low demand

This leads us to look briefly at issues affecting the demand for housing from the perspective of a variety of scales. Debates about housing clearly need to start from a national perspective (indeed, they may also need to recognise an international perspective on economic and social change). However, many of the more localised issues sit uncomfortably at these higher levels. They fail to be sufficiently understood or relevant when considered generally across the country. Therefore, housing and urban policy-makers have often found it necessary to move down through regional, district and neighbourhood levels to fully understand housing issues.

Starting with the visible symptoms of low and changing demand – turnover, empty properties, low prices – the local level is clearly highly significant, yet it may be the most problematic to consistently define. Where precisely can we say the locus of low demand is? Individual houses, streets and estates are the first and most obvious answer, but there are many examples of demand differences that defy spatial logic at very local levels. Many people can point readily to parts of cities where residents of popular and unpopular neighbourhoods live cheek by jowl. For these reasons, the concept of 'neighbourhood' is a particularly useful one in terms of understanding peoples' perceptions, particularly as and when they make housing decisions – yet, even so, neighbourhoods remain notoriously problematic to define. They may lie awkwardly in between estates and streets, may vary according to socio-economic status or age, or for the purposes for which they are being defined. Indeed, as Galster (2001) contends, neighbourhoods may not even be spatially bounded but, rather, consist of a more abstract confluence of attributes:

Neighbourhood is the bundle of spatially based attributes associated with clusters of residences, sometimes in conjunction with other land uses (Galster, 2001, p.2112).

A neighbourhood defined in this way is likely to vary wildly in size according to local context and in response to demand concepts like popularity. It is partly to circumvent these definitional problems – but also in acceptance of Galster's arguments – that some researchers and policy-makers have reasoned that the basic units of analysis should not be streets or estates, or indeed neighbourhoods. For many, the market context of the problem dictates that there is no alternative than to study the 'atoms' that make up the housing market: individual dwellings and households. Within this framework, the interactions of people, their homes, their decisions and constraints are of critical importance. How else can policy even begin to recognise situations such as that in the Welsh Streets in Liverpool where *Inside Housing* reported next-door neighbours that held diametrically opposing views about the merits of the demolition of their homes?[2]

This chapter cannot be concerned with the 'atoms' of the housing market yet, however. The minutiae of the housing market does not paint a very clear picture if we are unaware of its wider structure. Just as one has to stand back to observe the sense of a pointillist painting, we first need some idea of the broader structure – the patterns and constraints that impose themselves on human agency – before appreciating the detail. So, it is that we now consider some of the wider structural debates that were shaping the response to low demand towards the end of the 20th century.

Economic restructuring

As the Liverpool case study earlier in this chapter makes plain, one of the most powerful explanations for the problem of housing market weakness lies in the profound economic restructuring that had had serious and far reaching implications for the residential base of urban areas in the UK, over a long period of time. By the mid 1990s a serious gap in regional economic growth had emerged between the northern and southern regions of England. As can be seen from Figure 2.3 on the next page, changes in annual growth in gross value added (GVA) per capita – a measure of economic growth – in the northern regions had been broadly in step with London and the South East until about 1995. From this point on, a significant divergence for the North East and the North West is apparent, with Yorkshire and Humberside following about a year later. Although there was some degree of recovery in this pattern from 2001, when regional growth rates began to move broadly in step once again, the significant divergence in the late 1990s corresponded closely with the emergence of the low-demand problem.

---

2   'Welsh Streets demolition will go ahead', *Inside Housing*, 23 September 2005.

Figure 2.3: Annual growth in GVA per capita for selected regions, 1990-2005

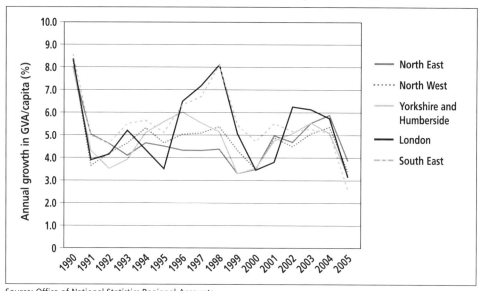

Source: Office of National Statistics Regional Accounts.

The divergence in economic growth rates in the late 1990s served to widen the existing gaps in absolute productivity between regions (Figure 2.4). This had an impact on the housing market. Mirroring the widening regional disparity in economic output, a significant divergence in house price growth between regions also opened up in the second half of the 1990s. While the impact of the recession and housing market crash earlier that decade was most severe in the South of the country, London and the southern regions recovered more quickly than their northern counterparts (Figure 2.5). For nearly the whole decade, northern regions experienced either decline or only single-digit growth in average house prices. A correction since has been short lived.

By 1998, many commentators in Britain were deeply worried that the UK was witnessing the onset of US-style 'rust belt' abandonment. At a conference in York that was convened to discuss the problem, David Webster demonstrated the connection between unemployment and housing surpluses in areas of the country where there were population losses (Webster, 1998). In attempting to synthesise possible responses to the dilemma, he could envisage only two. First of these was effectively the state-sponsored endorsement of the abandonment of urban areas (a move that was most certainly contrary to recommendations of the Urban Task Force). The second was the state-assisted reversal of the decentralisation of people and jobs. Of the two, he concluded that the latter might have been a more realistic response than had previously been given credit. *'The emphasis,'* he said, *'...should generally be on rebuilding the blue collar employment base of low income neighbourhoods in the cities and coalfields'* (p.47).

Figure 2.4: GVA per capita for selected regions, 1990-2005

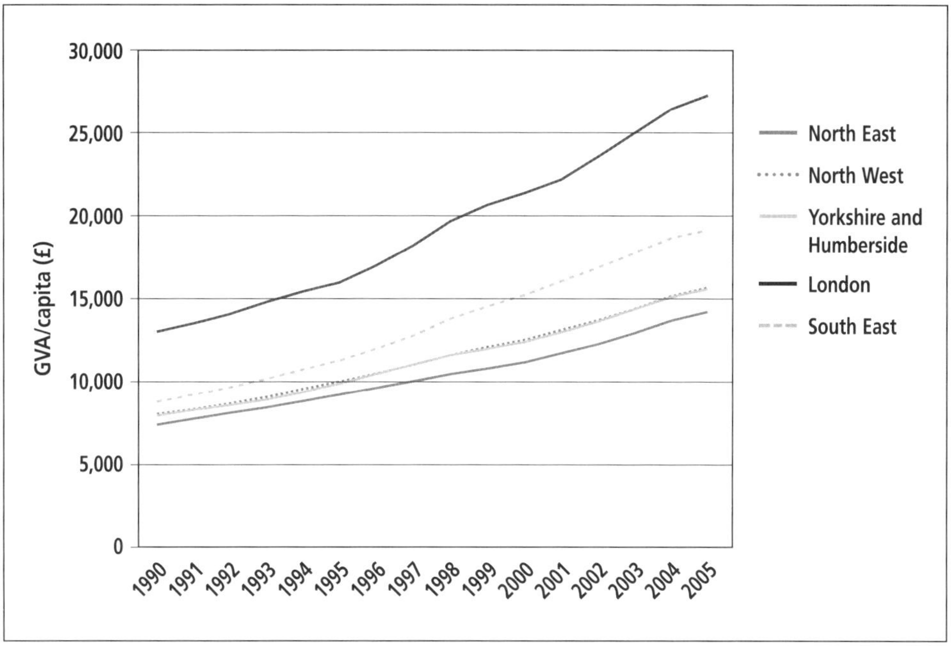

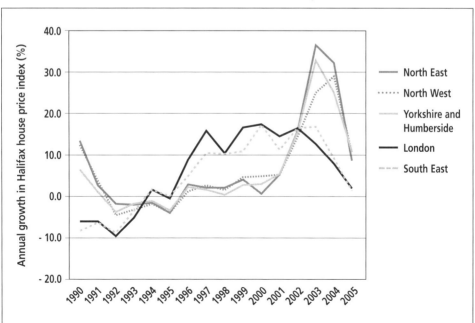

Source: Office of National Statistics Regional Accounts.

Figure 2.5: Annual growth in house sale prices for selected regions, 1990-2005

Source: HBOS plc.

It can be recalled that the redistribution of jobs around the country was an explicit economic policy following the Second World War. It was closely tied to the country's emerging land use planning infrastructure and rather pessimistic post-war estimates of economic growth. Industrial Development Certificates (IDCs) provided the government with a mechanism by which it could influence the spatial location of investment in new manufacturing. Ultimately, however, these measures seemed increasingly at odds with the need for competitiveness in a globalising economy and, in any case, economic and population growth throughout the 1950s appeared to undermine the argument that planners needed controls to mitigate against the effects of zero growth. If, as Cullingworth and Nadin (1994) have pointed out, post-war planning policy was predicated on only '...*modest economic growth, little population increase...little migration*...[and] *a balance in economic activity among the regions*' (p.11), then it is clear that some of the *raisons d'être* of a policy of economic redistribution no longer applied. Additionally, the decline of manufacturing, and the growth in its place of a more diffuse service-based economy that was largely office-based, meant that the IDC system became a less effective and less relevant tool. Critics could argue that the same would apply today.

But, what of the first of Webster's options? Again, there are clear precedents where the state has effectively recognised economic obsolescence and planned for some form of 'managed decline'. The example of the Durham County Plan of 1951, with its categorisation of settlements according to their economic and population prospects, is well known. Its policy of 'D villages' (which were to be demolished) was conceived of as a rational response to a serious decline in mining employment and was widely opposed by residents (Pattison 2004). Indeed, Pattison's history of the local reportage of the time reveals fears and concerns that are strongly echoed in some of the resistance to demolition in today's Pathfinder areas (see Chapter 5):

> *I've spent about £500 to £600 on this house and I'm not the only one...If the houses were in a condemned state I could understand. But they are not. Yes we are certainly going to fight the Council if they try to flatten our houses...We have spent over £400 on this house and been in only five years. We have used all our savings to put it right. We don't want to move* ('No Flattening our "Bleak, Neat Village" Storm "This is Our Home"', *Northern Echo*, 18 December 1963, quoted in Pattison, 2004, p.320).

Although similar stories can be told about households in today's low-demand areas, it would be inaccurate to say that opposition was the only response to plans for market renewal. In some areas, the local and regional media were broadly supportive of plans for demolition and clearance, and similar enthusiasm could also be found among sections of the general public. In May 2002, almost two years prior to the publication of the North Staffordshire Pathfinder (Renew) prospectus, the Stoke *Sentinel* ran a front page in support of recommendations for large-scale clearance made to the North Staffordshire housing and regeneration partnership.

Figure 2.6: Headlines in the Stoke *Sentinel* supporting demolition of properties and supported by the local population

Source: *The Sentinel*, Stoke on Trent, Monday 20 May 2002 and Thursday 26 September 2002.

This was followed up less than 6 months later when the same newspaper published a MORI poll of residents in Stoke on Trent, Newcastle under Lyme and the Staffordshire Moorlands which appeared to demonstrate wide support for demolition and restructuring: 82 per cent of respondents to the poll supported demolition and rebuilding parts of the city and 73 per cent were in favour of clearing parts of council estates (see Figure 2.6).

Such headlines demonstrated the very real and intractable problems of individual property rights and the meaning of 'home' conflicting with a 'rational' policy aiming for some 'collective good' – a theme that lies at the heart of the practical problems that face practitioners in their attempts to intervene in the housing market. Balancing individual rights against some articulation of the collective good is probably the central philosophical conundrum in all planning and regeneration policy, and no more so than with HMR.

HMR is in a good position to learn how to sensitively balance these conflicting needs, and given all its precedents and their lessons, the policy is challenged by the media and residents alike. But, despite its unpopularity, demolition, as Webster (1998) noted, will always remain an option. As is often the case, the devil is likely to reside in the detail: demographics, residents' aspirations, local housing and labour market conditions all vary from place to place and there can be no automatic assumption therefore that demolition is the appropriate policy response in all cases.

Returning to the 1990s, but with clear echoes of the Durham experience, Cole *et al.* (1999) were left in no doubt that housing practitioners were of necessity engaged in a process of 'managing decline,' although they found that most housing providers avoided the use of such emotive language when describing their activities. While economic restructuring provides one of the most convincing explanations for the low-demand phenomenon, intense sensitivities meant that economic arguments for the response were much less appropriate and ran the real risk of riding roughshod over valid local considerations. This is a central dilemma in a 'rescaled' policy environment: when local housing is reconceptualised as a regional asset, the question of balancing local and regional priorities inevitably moves to the centre of the stage. As Pattison (2004) pragmatically concluded, demolition '...reflects an approach to planning that pursued a single line of thought at the expense of other possibilities' (p.327).

The links between housing and the economy

As the data on regional productivity shown above suggest, regional differentials in the economy are an important driver of housing market conditions. Yet, the precise links are probably too complex to be adequately captured by a regional analysis. As Turok and Edge (1999) showed in their analysis of the 'jobs gap' between different cities in Britain, by the end of the 21st century there had been a significant divergence in the economic fortunes of different types of area. They concluded that the UK's conurbations and major urban agglomerations had fared much worse than rural areas or relatively 'free-standing' cities such as Nottingham and Edinburgh. Where there had been an improvement in city economies, the sustainability of those improvements was often open to question. Moreover, the residential and commuting patterns associated with economic growth were usually to the detriment of the older cores of those cities. Large-scale Foreign Direct Investment (FDI) projects in northern regions had clearly had some impact, but the most recent concerns about the long-term viability of this investment in the face of global corporate restructuring, together with a sectoral shift towards lower-paid, casual forms of work, have serious implications for sustainability. This was potently demonstrated in the North East in the closure of the Siemens semi-conductor plant, a vaunted inward-investment project, barely into the second year of its operation (Kirchner, 2000). Although startling, this was not an isolated incident: the 'global downturn' associated with the bursting of the dot-com bubble in the late 1990s saw job losses continue unabated as manufacturing capital continued to migrate towards cheaper labour markets. Even in the stronger economy of the 2000s, there continued to be examples of closures, particularly of manufacturing facilities, that demonstrated the dispensability of capital assets and hinted at the fragility of regional economic strategies that were over-reliant on FDI.

Economic change was (and continues to be) apparent at the local level as well. As we have seen, profound changes to the economic structure within cities have occurred over the course of the second half of the 20th century. These can be linked to the changing fortunes of neighbourhoods and their housing. Power and Mumford (1999) described cases of the abandonment of housing in Newcastle upon Tyne and Manchester, concluding that such abandonment was the extreme outcome of a process whereby inner city areas had lost jobs (due to downgrading of traditional industrial and manufacturing industries, relocation to the urban periphery and closure of branch establishments), and where those who had remained employed exercised the choice to move away. Many areas of low demand were, they found, characterised by thinned-out, low-income populations where poverty was well above the national average and almost half the population of working age was outside the labour market or education.

Access to local jobs and training are essential for the stability of communities. Economic change left many former industrial settlements bereft of local employment opportunities and in many cases new jobs, where they could be found, were insecure and low paid – a situation that continues to challenge deprived communities. The new, growing sectors demanded skills and employee attributes that were a poor match for former employees of declining industries such as shipbuilding, steelmaking and mining. These new sectors also demanded greater flexibility of their workforce. Access to local labour markets for some sections of the community is dependent on adequate and cost-effective local facilities such as childcare and skills training. Hilary Third (1995) found evidence that many unemployed mothers could not consider returning to work unless the full costs of childcare could be met – yet public services such as these in many low-demand areas were often patchy or weak as a falling population made it more difficult for local authorities to sustain them.

There is an even more direct consequence of economic change and worklessness. Work on housing benefit reform undertaken by Peter Kemp in the late 1990s found that there were disincentives associated with finding employment because it could often mean that eligibility for full housing benefit would be withdrawn (Kemp 1998). He found that this was having the effect of artificially inflating the numbers of households that were eligible for, and claiming, 100 per cent housing benefit. Furthermore, as is discussed later, he found that such households tended to have a very transient mode of housing consumption, with short tenancies and high turnover, usually (although not exclusively) in social housing and assisted by the portability of housing benefit.

The regional response

The emergence of the low-demand issue also coincided with a heightened interest in regional governance, which was being championed by John Prescott MP as deputy prime minister (Prescott, of course would go on to play a pivotal role in supporting HMR through his commitment to the Sustainable Communities Plan). The rise in regionalism, particularly through the creation of Regional Development Agencies (RDAs) in 1999 and revisions to Regional Planning Guidance (RPG), provided a timely mechanism for providing a regional perspective on housing supply and demand.

Although RDAs were set up with responsibility for driving regional economic development, their remit also included many aspects of physical regeneration. While initially there was little involvement of housing organisations in the development of RDAs (Long, 1999; Robinson, 2003), linkages subsequently became more developed. The role of RDAs is important because of the clear links between regional economic performance and the housing market.

But, it has always been understood – now even more so – that housing cannot just be a reactive element to regional economic strategy. Economic development and inward investment should capitalise on existing housing resources, particularly in areas of low demand. More recently, the nascent city regions have been explicit in their recognition of the contribution that good quality housing and neighbourhoods can make. The house building industry was even more direct when it extolled the importance of housing in 1999:

> [T]*he provision of the right kind of housing in the right places is a key element of the infrastructure needed to stimulate investment and jobs* (HBF, undated, p.1).

At the height of the concern about low demand, the House Builders' Federation (HBF) attacked the draft RPG for the North East as being a document that was primarily concerned with managing decline. Their argument was that, while the regional planners and the RDA (One NorthEast) were aiming for economic growth, their approach to housing provision – a policy to regenerate the urban cores – was inconsistent with this (see Counsell and Haughton, 2003 for a detailed account). Closer concordance between regional planning and housing strategy is now an accepted fact of life and it is clear that some compromise has been possible. Today, a central plank of most Pathfinders' strategies is addressing the 'monolithic' or unvarying nature of the housing profile in low-demand areas. Particular attention is drawn to the lack of 'aspirational' housing pathways to encourage, among other things, the retention of graduates, Black and Minority Ethnic (BME) groups, and other groups of increasing affluence who are able to exercise increasing choice in the market. Thus, the HBF's plea for 'the right kind of housing in the right areas' has been heard – the danger now is that further growth favours suburban and freestanding settlements and could lead to a repeat of the over-supply problem. Furthermore, the house building industry's tendency to latch onto ideas (such as one- and two-bedroomed city centre apartments), to the cost of a more balanced approach to provision is another risk in this vein.

Demography and population mobility

At the same time as economic change, there were also demographic changes that were fundamentally changing the nature of demand for housing. This section focuses on how the demographic composition of demand for housing altered, exacerbating the other structural drivers of change that were apparent in the housing market. Part of this demographic shift was accounted for by migration. Patterns of residential mobility – in response partly to economic change, partly to increased housing market opportunities – were found to be important factors underpinning the changing demand for housing.

The changing profile of residents

Alongside changes in the economic structure of cities, there have been significant changes in the profile of households and residents, both in social housing and in the private sector. The 'residualisation' of social housing was a dominant theme in the literature of the early 1980s, bound to the massive social and political changes that the decade was ushering in. Residualisation – whereby social housing (council housing in particular) moved away from being a tenure of choice capable of meeting general needs towards being a 'safety-net' for only the least well-off – represented not only a new political agenda of centralisation and weakening of the local government (and hence local modes of provision – see for example, Wolman, 1995), but also a changing culture of ownership and self-reliance (Mullins, 1998). Ray Forrest and Alan Murie (1983) have long argued that the broader social, economic and political forces leading to residualisation were over and above local issues of housing management and process.

Allied to this, tenants were increasingly not viewing social housing as a tenure for life. This was particularly the case for new entrants to social housing, who tended to be younger and living in smaller households. In explaining the emergence of the low-demand problem, Roger Burrows found that 72 per cent of households entering the social rented sector in 1993/94 were headed by someone aged under 30, and tenants were more likely to be lone parents, unemployed, or both. By the same year, the demographic structure of the social rented sector had changed so much that it was clearly both an 'old' and a 'young' tenure at the same time (Burrows 1999; see also Figure 2.7 on the next page). Many housing providers were clearly concerned that a high proportion of their tenants were elderly and would die or require specialist care – and that the replacement tenants were more transient and, given the choice, would be unlikely to remain in the sector. The prognosis was for continuing falls in the demand for social rented housing and higher turnover. As a precursor to HMR, for example, Sheffield City Council had been attracting considerable attention since the late 1990s by demolishing an average of around 2,000 council homes a year to bring supply more in line with perceived future demand.

Indeed, this prognosis appears to have been borne out. A key part of John Hills' (2007) analysis of the future of the social rented sector demonstrates how the age profile of the sector has, to paraphrase his words, 'flattened out' (p.49). As can be seen in Figure 2.8, the spike of retirement-age householders has reduced somewhat, leaving the sector much younger in profile than it was. Additionally, the very young cohort of entrants identified in Burrows' analysis appears to have aged into their 30s and 40s. At one level this suggests a sector that, while facing problems of internal turnover, is still not sufficiently attracting new tenants or facilitating normal levels of inter-tenure mobility.

Figure 2.7: The age distribution of heads of household in the social rented sector, 1993/94

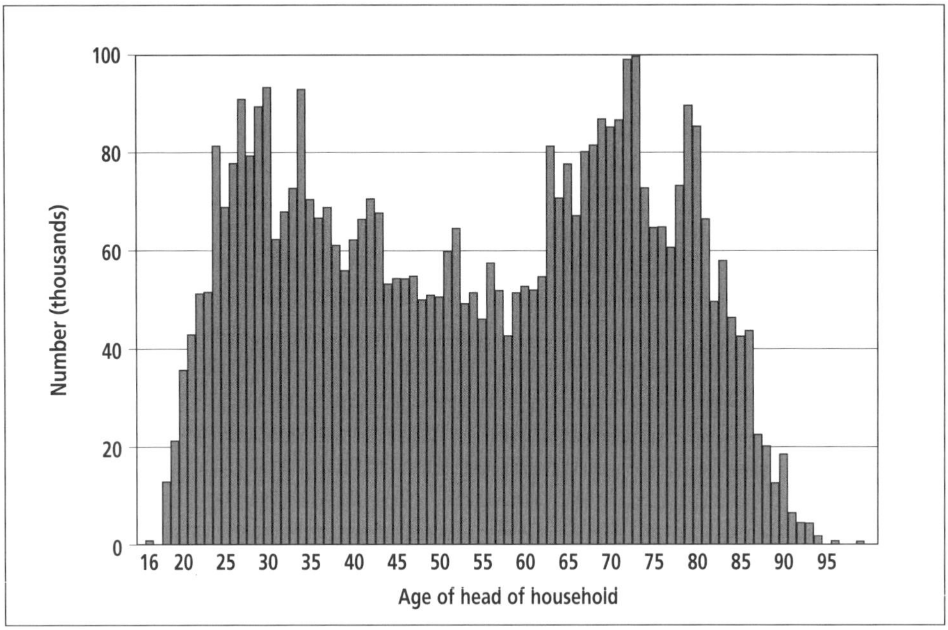

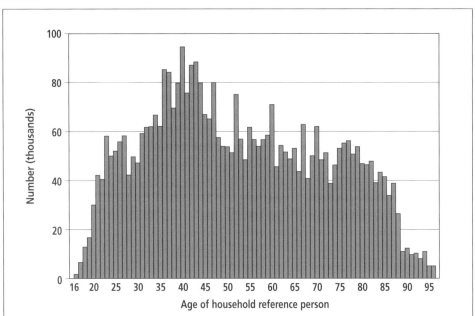

Source: Survey of English Housing; Burrows (1999).

Figure 2.8: The age distribution of household reference persons in the social rented sector, 2007/08

Source: authors' analysis of the Survey of English Housing.

Summary

In this chapter we have traced the evolution of the low and changing demand debate. Changes in demand resulted from a combination of macro and micro-level factors, operating across different time periods. The mismatch, or asymmetry, between housing and labour markets is evidenced by the lag between processes of deindustrialisation and decentralisation in planning that began in the 1960s and 1970s, changes in housing policy such as the right to buy and the introduction of 'portable' housing benefits which occurred in the 1970s and 1980s, and the emergence of low and changing demand for housing which surfaced in the 1990s. The importance of scale, and the requirement that housing, planning and regeneration professionals develop a greater degree of spatial literacy in the design and implementation of policies, is reflected in the increasing level of integration at regional level between housing, economic and planning strategies during the past decade. The complexity of interaction between housing and labour markets, and the asymmetry between them, makes foresight and future strategic development at these spatial scales a priority for investment. In the next chapter we consider the way in which the evidence was brought to bear on the need for intervention in housing markets to deal with this perceived asymmetry.

CHAPTER 3:
Establishing the need:
the evidence base for
policy innovation

Introduction

In Chapter 1 we suggested that the question of renewing and delivering sustainable housing markets required the adoption of a perspective on housing's broader social and economic role. We contended that a 'rescaling' of housing – local housing being expropriated as assets for regional economic competitiveness – had been joined with a concern for the role of 'place' in reproducing processes of social exclusion. These perspectives, which we asserted were characteristic of New Labour policy in the late 1990s, arguably demanded new approaches to the analysis of housing and its role in inner urban areas and conurbations, and to the conceptualisation of housing 'need'. The mantra of 'evidence-based policy', which pervaded policy formulation at the time, also required a more sophisticated approach, able to reconcile the 'scale' and 'dynamics' of processes affecting the housing market in low and changing demand neighbourhoods, some of which were reviewed in Chapter 2.

This third chapter focuses on the evidence that was assembled to develop this new understanding of housing, its role and its scale of influence. We show how an emerging evidence base was marshalled to support the innovation of new policy responses, ultimately giving rise to the HMR concept. We examine the methodology and results of a number of key studies that established the evidence base related to HMR. Significant among these studies was the suite of regional analyses undertaken by the University of Birmingham's Centre for Urban and Regional Studies (CURS) between 2000 and 2003. In these studies, the concept of areas 'at risk' of housing market change was advanced, and this formed the backbone of analytical approaches that simultaneously examined geographic scale and the possibilities of market change over time.

In the chapter, reference is made to each of the regions of the Midlands and North of England and, in so doing, we aim to: (i) bring together the separate regional studies of changing demand published by CURS in the period 2000-2003; (ii) present the development of the methodology for identifying areas at risk of low and changing demand used in a number of regional and local studies on low demand and housing market change, and (iii) provide a commentary on the 'areas at risk' analysis and comment on its implications for policy.

In summary, this chapter will:

- Report on the spatial pattern of 'risk' of changing demand for the whole of the North and Midlands of England.
- Assess the relationship between the risk of low demand and housing tenure.
- Review how the identification of risk relates to the nine Housing Market Renewal Pathfinders.
- Highlight local factors that affect low and changing demand.
- Provide illustrations of local case studies used to understand housing markets for investment and strategic purposes.

Whilst the regional research on low and changing demand has been typically aimed at local and regional policy-makers, the length of these reports and the detailed technical work behind the analysis of the 'areas at risk' of changing demand has limited the potential for dissemination to a wider policy and research audience. We hope, therefore, that this chapter will provide a useful reference point for future work in this area, especially in the light of continuing improvements in the availability of small area statistics on the housing and socio-economic characteristics of neighbourhoods, and of the skills to analyse and interpret these.

Background

Low and changing demand for housing joined affordability as one of the most important housing problems facing England at the start of the 21st century. By the turn of the century in some areas of the North and Midlands, house prices were at best static and in some cases were falling substantially in real terms. The demand for social rented housing had substantially weakened. In some cases, this had led to very high localised void levels, high turnover (Keenan, 1998; Pawson and Bramley, 2000) and, in extreme cases, dwelling abandonment (Keenan *et al.*, 1999; Power and Mumford, 1999).

In many areas, neighbourhoods experiencing low or changing demand were to be found close to other neighbourhoods where prices were continuing to rise, and where affordability in the private market or access to limited social rented housing resources were problems of serious local concern. All of those regions most affected by low and changing demand had areas where affordability problems were also high on the agenda. What emerged in the private market was a more differentiated pattern of prices, with certain areas and types of property falling out of the general pattern of price appreciation. This fragmentation of the private housing market was entirely consistent with Forrest *et al.*'s (1990) analysis of the problems associated with the expansion of owner-occupation at the cost of the rental housing. The spatial patterning and scale of local housing market conditions became an important aspect of analytic and policy concern.

In social rented housing, however, there was a more widespread decline in demand, particularly from potential new entrants to the sector. There was also a change in perceptions of the extent to which the sector could provide a long-term housing solution, especially among young people. This was often compounded by pre-existing local perceptions of the attractiveness of particular estates. This pattern of changing aspirations was reflected in the characteristics of households entering and leaving social housing, as we described in Chapter 2. For those leaving the sector, location and desire to move to a 'better neighbourhood' were important drivers of turnover.

A new problem?

One of the key features of the debate around low and changing demand was an agreement that problematic market conditions were the result of a complex interplay of national, regional, sub-regional and local factors. In this sense, the problem was seen to be quite different from that of 'difficult-to-let' social rented housing, or, problems associated with older private sector housing in need of renewal. There was a recognition that any attempt to achieve a measurement of the risk of low or changing demand needed to account for a diversity of factors at play, including those at wider spatial scale. The low and changing demand debate was, in some respects, about the 'fit' between a housing stock that had evolved (and in some cases had been planned wholesale) to serve particular local needs on the one hand and, on the other, the changing demands and aspirations of contemporary households whose lives were playing out over wider spaces against a backdrop of a changed economic context.

A key part of the rationale for a strong policy intervention was the prevalence of empty and unused residential property. The problems or risk of outright abandonment were perhaps never as severe as in the North American context, but the worry was real: see Keenan *et al.* (1999). Vacancy rates in comparable US cities in 2000 frequently exceeded one in ten properties. Baltimore (13.7 per cent), Pittsburgh (11.5 per cent), Cleveland (11.4 per cent) and Detroit (10.2 per cent), were among the most afflicted of the USA's ex-industrial cities (HUD, 2000). Areas of significant market weakness in England were also characterised by high vacancy rates, if not as high as those in the US. Indeed, it was the government's inquiry into the problem of empty homes (HC 240-I, 2001-02), which found evidence of over 750,000 vacant residential properties in England in 2000, that prompted the establishment of a Housing Market Renewal Fund. Some improvement in the empty homes situation has been apparent since the HMR programme was set up. In 2002, local authority areas participating in the HMR programme had an average vacancy rate of 5.2 per cent, compared with the England average of 3.4 per cent (Leather *et al.*, 2007). By 2007, the same areas had an average of 4.4 per cent, significantly closer to the England average of 3.1 per cent (see Figure 5.3 in Chapter 5).

Yet it is difficult to disentangle the effect of economic change that is reflected in these crude averages from the outcomes of other processes. As an interesting counterpoint to the low-demand phenomenon, many cities are now growing increasingly anxious about very high vacancy rates in their renascent city centres: Sprigings *et al.* (2006) note the importance of speculative activity in explaining high vacancy rates in city centre apartment developments. Their paper cites evidence in Liverpool that around 13 per cent of city centre dwellings were vacant, and anecdote would suggest that this may be a conservative estimate. Recently, DTZ (2007) found at least 6.5 per cent of similar properties in Sheffield had been empty for over six months and that vacancy rates in some schemes were as high as 50 per cent. Empty residential properties in these very 'specialised' parts of the market will distort district-wide averages.

Local factors such as the reputation of the area, crime and anti-social behaviour, urban design issues and the quality, design and condition of the housing stock have had an obvious impact on the popularity of housing and neighbourhoods. But, these local factors are contextualised by wider, structural factors. As we saw earlier, there was an increasing recognition that broader societal processes such as demographic trends, changing aspirations regarding tenure and property type, the structure of housing benefits, planning policies, and the state of the macro-economy were having, directly or indirectly, an influence on housing demand and, in extreme cases, were leading to the abandonment of housing and neighbourhoods in the North and Midlands (see Murie *et al.*, 1998; Pawson and Bramley, 2000).

Conversely, in economically buoyant regions such as London and the South East, although the structural conditions were more favourable, local factors such as economic and demographic change, or anti-social behaviour, resulted in a change in demand for particular neighbourhoods or estates. These factors, as well as features of dwelling type, size design and location, contributed towards some areas in London and the South being less popular and more exposed to the problems associated with higher turnover – but there was not the diagnosis of widespread 'low demand' as experienced in the North and Midlands. Localised unpopularity did not translate into the sort of market weakness and abandonment witnessed in northern regions because the South's markets remained generally 'overheated', imposing limits on the choices that households could ultimately make.

Identifying areas at risk of changing demand

It was against this background of housing market change and an increasing concern about its urban policy implications that a number of local authorities and housing associations in the North and Midlands began to commission research to identify areas at risk of changing demand. Between 1999 and 2003 the Centre for Urban and Regional Studies (CURS) at the University of Birmingham was commissioned by a number of regional partnerships to undertake several regional, sub-regional and local studies of low and changing demand. A distinctive spatial analysis of the risk associated with changing demand – which is set out in this chapter – was developed over the course of these studies.

While there were by this time a number of studies of low demand, the sociological and phenomenological insights that these afforded nevertheless left some basic questions about the scale and geography of the problem unanswered. The PAT 7 study undertaken by researchers at Heriot-Watt University provided some robust data on how widespread the problem was nationally and regionally, and was useful in beginning to chart out some of the factors underpinning the problem locally. But, it did not undertake a detailed spatial analysis of how the problem affected neighbourhoods. Conversely, Power and Mumford's (1999) case studies of abandonment explained a great deal about the impact of processes of urban decline and vicious cycles of policy withdrawal and disinvestment, but they could not be used to extrapolate across the regional scale. The aim, then, of the CURS work was to develop a diagnostic tool that could help to clarify the scale and extent of the problem and which could help policy-makers to develop and prioritise a costed programme of interventions.

Given the multi-dimensional and multi-scalar nature of the problem, it is not surprising that no single data source or underlying factor was isolated as an effective measure of low demand. For example:

- **Local labour markets:** Although the loss of local employment may weaken demand, the attractiveness of properties or locations may mean that the effect is not significant in the short to medium term.
- **The local economy:** An improvement in the economy may not forestall a weakening of demand for certain tenures, property types or neighbourhoods as it may increase the capacity for households to exit low-cost rental sectors. This happened in the North West during the 1990s, where demand for social housing fell in line with the unemployment rate for the region (see Nevin, Lee *et al.*, 2000). Economic indicators in themselves may not be an effective guide to changing demand at the local level.
- **Poverty and deprivation:** In some circumstances a high concentration of deprivation may reflect a particularly segregated housing market. Demand from lower-income households, particularly Black and Minority Ethnic (BME) communities, may support the local housing market in certain neighbourhood types, for example inner city areas. This partly helps to explain why in some parts of London and the South East deprivation and high demand were (and remain) co-existent. Therefore it follows that official indicators of poverty such as the Index of Multiple Deprivation are not by themselves sufficient indicators of low demand.
- **Empty properties:** Although high rates of void properties demonstrate a general weakness of local demand, particularly when properties have been persistently empty over long periods of time (e.g., over six months), there are also other reasons why houses remain empty. It must always be borne in

mind that a normally functioning housing market will need to have a proportion of its stock empty as a consequence of normal market transactions, improvements, or speculative strategies. A long-term vacancies indicator partly accounts for this, for example, properties empty for more than six months, although this by itself does not entirely capture the low-demand phenomenon.

- **Housing conditions:** Whilst housing quality can be an important local determinant of demand it is difficult to assemble data at a consistent basis for regional and sub-regional analysis and minimum fitness or decency standards are not necessarily a good measure of quality. High profile examples of new, high quality developments suffering from low demand raised significant questions about the link between quality and demand. Furthermore, in pressurised market contexts, there may be healthy demand even for lower quality housing.
- **Housing types:** Whilst certain dwelling types are more likely to be unpopular (e.g., those of non-traditional construction, one bedroom flats, or older small terraces), none of these categories is unpopular in all cases and much depends on local market dynamics and wider neighbourhood characteristics.

More appropriate data may exist within individual organisations, but the analyses that are required at the regional and sub-regional levels need to draw upon data that exist in the same form across different areas and organisations. As a result of these limitations, many regional and sub-regional studies have tended to rely on data from the ten-yearly population censuses. Despite some limitations, the use of data from the 1991 and then 2001 censuses allowed a consistent national picture of the variables most associated with problematic demand conditions to be built up. This analysis formed a starting point for identifying a 'coalescence of risk', across local authority boundaries. Policy-makers became more concerned with large areas over which the same problems were occurring, rather than small, isolated areas. The variables used were indicators of demand – 'risk factors' – and individually are subject to caveats of the types mentioned above. It is their combined use, however, that serves to produce a more robust picture of risk than they would individually.

The CURS studies of 'risk'

The first regional report to identify areas 'at risk' of low or changing demand at the small area level was published by CURS in 2001. Entitled *Changing Housing Markets and Urban Regeneration in the M62 Corridor*, the report was commissioned by a consortium of local authorities in the North West together with the Housing Corporation and Northern Consortium of Housing Authorities. The report detailed the development of a method to identify areas 'at risk' of low or changing demand by computing a 'risk' index at small area level (using census enumeration districts[3]) across the 18 contiguous local authorities along the M62 from Wirral to Oldham (west to east), and between Blackburn and Halton (north to south) (Figure 3.1).

---

3 The original report was based on the 1991 census and used 'enumeration districts' (EDs) as the basis for analysis. EDs typically contained around 200 households. EDs were superceded in the 2001 census by 'output areas' (OAs).

Figure 3.1: The 'M62 report' study area

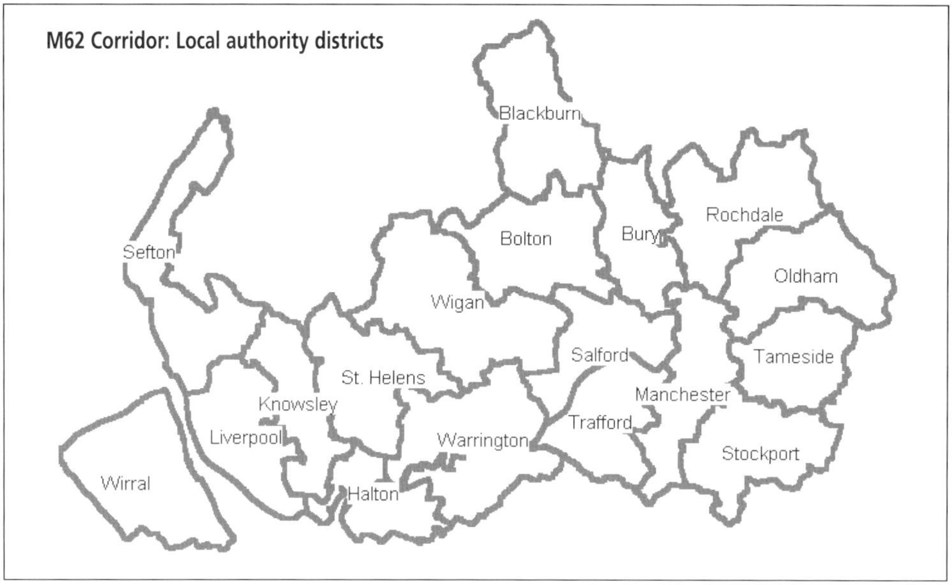

M62 Corridor: Local authority districts

Blackburn
Rochdale
Bolton
Bury
Sefton
Oldham
Wigan
Salford
Tameside
St. Helens
Manchester
Knowsley
Trafford
Liverpool
Warrington
Stockport
Wirral
Halton

Source: Nevin, Lee *et al.* (2000).

The basic calculation of risk combined five indicators of factors known to be associated with low demand. The indicators were standardised using a chi-square index. Previous research (Lee *et al.*, 1995) had shown this method to be most resistant to error at the small area level. Essentially, 'risk' was the sum of chi-square indices of five variables drawn from the census:

1. **Proportion of population that was economically inactive (excluding retired).**
2. **Proportion of economically active population that was unemployed:** These two indicators were used to measure concentrations of economic inactivity (excluding normal retirement). Indirectly, the indicators could be seen to be related to the extent to which households with choice may have left the area, or not moved in to the area. The lack of disposable income among affected households has an impact, among other things, on their ability to maintain housing in good condition. The reduced chances of retention of future generations in such areas, given poor stock conditions and a reduced economic outlook, increase the risk of future incidence of low demand.
3. **Proportion of population that was aged 65 or over:** This demographic indicator was included as this relates to the chances that an area will suffer future depopulation due to an ageing resident base.
4. **Proportion of dwellings that were flats:** In areas of low demand, households with means are able to exercise an increased level of choice. In this context, flats become relatively unpopular compared to other dwelling types.

Whilst this may not in itself be indicative of demand problems, a concentration of one type of dwelling in an area – particularly a type with marginal popularity such as flats – was seen to increase that area's exposure to future problems.

5. **Proportion of dwellings that were terrace houses:** Research carried out in problem market areas in Yorkshire and Humberside (Lee, Hall *et al.*, 2002; Lee, Leather, Murie *et al.*, 2002) and the West Midlands (Nevin, Lee *et al.*, 2001), showed that the prices of terrace housing had failed to keep pace with those of other types of dwelling. Many low-demand areas were characterised by having a stock profile in which terrace housing was particularly over-represented.

Each indicator was weighted equally. Full details of the derivation of the chi-square indices and their combination can be found in Appendix 2. Indicators were also combined using a spatial analytic process aimed at examining the 'adjacency' of high scores. This essentially down-weighted isolated instances of risk, and up-weighted spatially contiguous coalescences of risk. A Geographical Information System (GIS), employing a process described fully in Appendix 3, was used to achieve this.

In subsequent studies (Leather *et al.*, 2002; Lee, Leather, Goodson *et al.*, 2002 and Lee, Leather, Murie *et al.*, 2002), further refinements were introduced. The most recent report at the regional level (Leather *et al.*, 2003) referred to a 3 stage process, with Stage 1 essentially replicating the original 'M62 study', and refinements referred to as Stages 2 and 3 introduced in these subsequent regional studies. In this chapter we bring together updated analyses for the North and Midlands for the first time. The three stages that we used in computing the risk index are set out below.

- **Stage 1:** The five risk factors were incorporated into an index using the process employed for the original M62 report, as described above. Updated data from the 2001 census were used. As before, indicators were standardised and a risk index of low or changing demand was computed for the whole of the North and Midlands.
- **Stage 2:** Areas that scored highly on the 'risk' index in Stage 1 (were above the median), but which did not score highly on the Index of Local Deprivation (were below the median), were filtered out. This was done because evidence suggests that deprivation is a precondition of weaker local housing markets, although the reverse is not necessarily true, i.e., not all deprived areas do or will suffer from low demand (see for example, Lee and Murie, 1997).
- **Stage 3:** In some areas, demand is related more to the local and regional economy, rather than local factors such as property type or even the demographics of the area's residents. To account for this, and to compensate for the lack of tenure differentiation in the main index, those areas with house prices above the regional median were filtered out.

The flowchart in Figure 3.2 sets out the broad logic that was applied to the combination of indicators in the calculation of the risk index. It is important to note that the results generated following the completion of the three stages should not be interpreted to imply that *all* properties in the areas identified are at risk. The value of the risk index gives an indication of the extent to which properties within the area may be considered to be at risk of low demand. Where there is a concentration of particular dwelling types, socio-economic characteristics, deprivation and low prices, this might indicate that significant housing market problems either already exist, or may be expected to arise in the future, unless policy action is taken to address the issue.

Figure 3.2: 'Risk' calculation flowchart

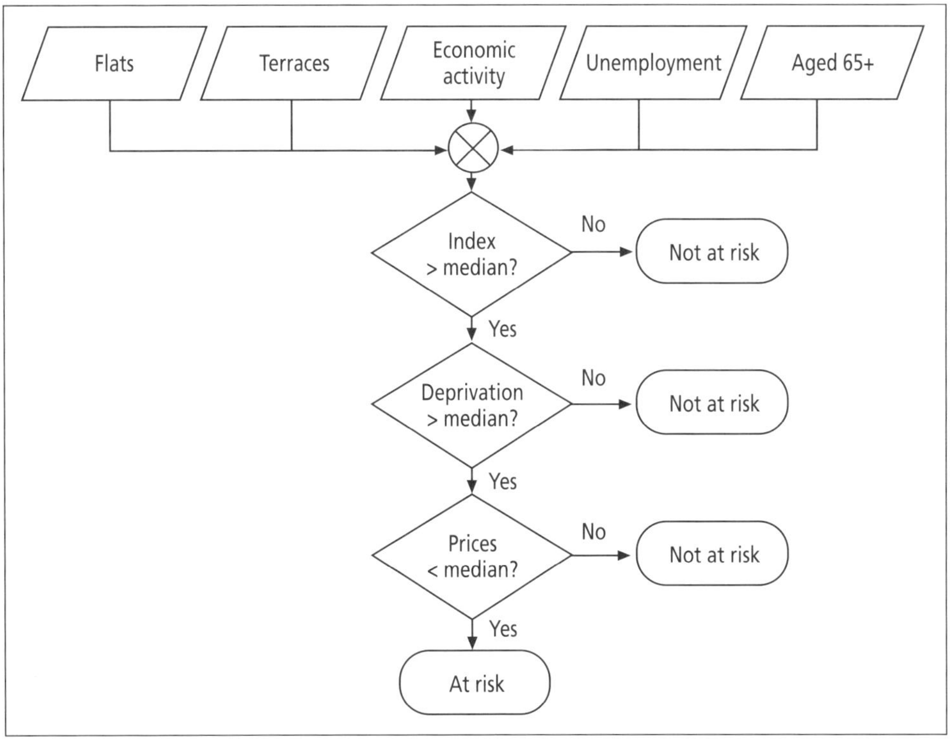

Source: authors' new analysis of CURS risk index.

Findings

Table 3.1 shows the breakdown of the 20 local authorities in the North and Midlands most exposed to problems of low and changing demand. The results do not imply that all properties in the areas identified are 'at risk'; however, the concentration of particular dwelling types and socio-economic characteristics do imply that there may be significant housing market problems in these local authority districts and that markets should be monitored for change.

Table 3.1: The 20 local authority districts with the highest degree of risk (Stage 3)

Local authority	Rank	No. of dwellings at risk	% of dwellings at risk
Easington	1	33,394	82.0
Kingston upon Hull	2	85,862	79.1
Wansbeck	3	19,512	74.5
Liverpool	4	141,579	72.0
South Tyneside	5	47,419	71.9
Knowsley	6	41,266	71.8
Wear Valley	7	19,349	71.6
Hartlepool	8	25,279	69.1
Derwentside	9	24,413	66.9
Sedgefield	10	24,431	65.9
Sandwell	11	78,619	65.7
Barnsley	12	57,281	63.0
Blackburn	13	34,508	62.5
Manchester	14	115,551	62.0
Hyndburn	15	20,308	61.9
Lincoln	16	22,437	61.8
Salford	17	61,110	61.5
Burnley	18	23,496	61.0
Sunderland	19	72,112	60.7
Leicester	20	66,865	59.7

Source: authors' new analysis of CURS risk index.

In a number of local authorities low demand was clearly manifest and reflected in the high and increasing incidence of vacant properties. For example, in Liverpool, the vacancy rate for the city was eight per cent (April 2001) but in the 'inner core' the vacancy rate averaged 30 per cent with as many as 8,000 properties empty (Lee and Nevin, 2002). In the inner core of Stoke on Trent the vacancy rate was 13 per cent in April 2002, representing approximately 2,300 properties (Lee, Leather, Goodson *et al.*, 2002).

The relative scale of the risk associated with changing demand was most significant in the North East of England: 82 per cent of dwellings in Easington, 75 per cent in Wansbeck, and 72 per cent of dwellings in South Tyneside were identified as at risk using the index. The problem was also severe in parts of Merseyside (Liverpool and Knowsley), Greater Manchester and Lancashire (Blackburn, Manchester, Hyndburn, Salford and Burnley), Yorkshire and the Humber (Hull and Barnsley), and the West Midlands (Stoke, the West Midlands conurbation and Coventry) (Table 3.1 and Figure 3.3).

Figure 3.3: Areas at risk of changing demand

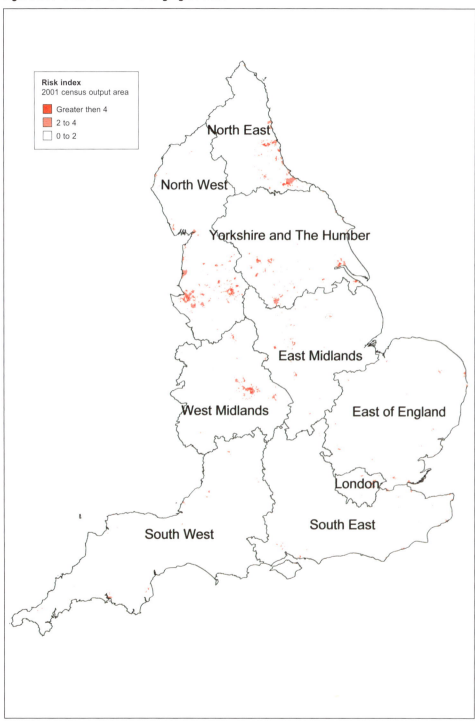

Source: authors' new analysis of CURS risk index.

Housing tenure and changing demand

Neighbourhoods at risk of low demand were predominantly those areas with a significant proportion of social housing. However, there remained clear evidence of the multi-tenure nature of housing market problems, with nearly 500,000 properties being privately owned in those areas identified as at risk in Table 3.1. Table 3.2 shows the extent of multi-tenure problems: the social rented sector is the majority tenure in areas at risk in Salford, Knowsley, Manchester, South Tyneside, Sunderland, Sandwell and Hull. In parts of Lancashire (Blackburn, Burnley and Hyndburn), it is the private sector that is most at risk, with social renting comprising only a minority of the dwellings in areas at risk. The private rented sector has a significant presence in Liverpool (12 per cent), Manchester (11 per cent), Hull (11 per cent), Lincoln (11 per cent), and Burnley (10 per cent), and the private sector is the dominant tenure in a significant number of local authorities. This evidence demonstrated that the areas at the greatest risk of low demand were often mixed tenure areas.

Table 3.2: Tenure characteristics of local authority districts with most dwellings in areas 'at risk'

	Social	Own	PRS
Salford	55.3	37.7	7.1
Knowsley	55.1	40.4	4.4
Manchester	54.5	34.6	10.9
South Tyneside	54.2	39.8	6.0
Sunderland	53.5	41.8	4.8
Sandwell	51.5	43.6	5.0
Hull	50.4	38.9	10.7
Sedgefield	47.9	48.8	3.3
Easington	47.8	47.8	4.3
Leicester	45.7	45.2	9.2
Liverpool	45.0	43.2	11.9
Barnsley	42.1	51.1	6.8
Hartlepool	41.6	51.3	7.1
Wear Valley	39.7	54.6	5.7
Wansbeck	39.6	53.5	6.9
Derwentside	39.6	56.1	4.3
Lincoln	38.2	51.2	10.6
Blackburn	37.6	56.8	5.6
Burnley	26.1	63.9	10.0
Hyndburn	21.8	70.0	8.2
Total	47.4	44.6	7.9

Source: authors' new analysis of CURS risk index.

Housing Market Renewal

The scale and cross-tenure nature of the problem was recognised by the government in its declaration of nine Housing Market Renewal (HMR) Pathfinders in April 2002. The Pathfinders were set up to take the lead on market restructuring by providing a focus on changing demand across broader housing market areas. The Pathfinders each encompassed between two and five neighbouring local authorities. Pathfinders were set up to cover significant parts of the metropolitan housing markets of Tyneside; East Lancashire; Oldham and Rochdale; Merseyside; Greater Manchester (two Pathfinders); East Yorkshire; South Yorkshire; Birmingham and the Black Country; and North Staffordshire. The precise location of these nine Pathfinders is shown in Figure 3.4 and the constituent local authorities are detailed in Table 3.3.

Table 3.3: The nine original Pathfinders

Region and area	Pathfinder name	Constituent local authority areas
North East (1 Pathfinder) • Tyneside	Bridging NewcastleGateshead (BNG)	• Gateshead • Newcastle upon Tyne
North West (4 Pathfinders) • East Lancashire	Elevate East Lancashire (EEL)	• Blackburn with Darwen • Burnley • Hyndburn • Pendle
• Greater Manchester (2 Pathfinders)	Manchester-Salford Partnership (MSP) Partners in Action (PiA)	• Manchester • Salford • Oldham • Rochdale
• Merseyside	NewHeartlands (NH)	• Liverpool • Sefton • Wirral
West Midlands (2 Pathfinders) • Birmingham and the Black Country	Urban Living (UL)	• Birmingham • Sandwell
• North Staffordshire	Renew North Staffordshire (RENEW)	• Newcastle under Lyme • Staffordshire Moorlands • Stoke on Trent
Yorkshire and the Humber (2 Pathfinders) • East Yorkshire	Gateway (GW)	• East Riding of Yorkshire • Kingston upon Hull
• South Yorkshire	Transform South Yorkshire (TSY)	• Barnsley • Doncaster • Rotherham • Sheffield
Total: 4 Regions	**9 Pathfinders**	**25 local authorities**

Figure 3.4: Relationship of 'risk' to HMRA Pathfinder areas

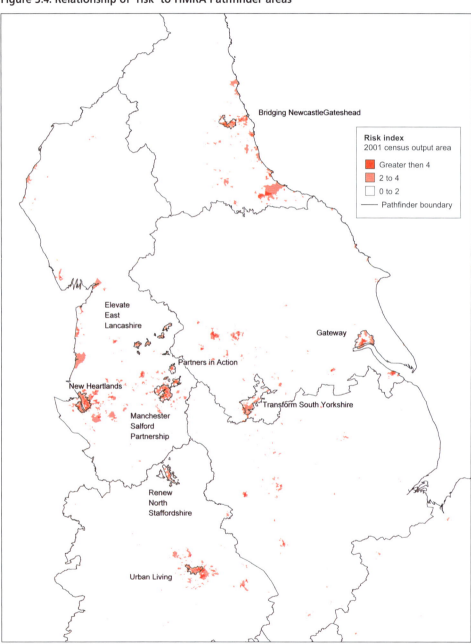

Source: authors' new analysis of CURS risk index.

The geographical 'footprint' of the original Pathfinders demonstrated a high degree of correlation with those areas identified as 'at risk' in the CURS reports on changing demand. They included areas with different problems, functions, and neighbourhoods with different trajectories. However, given the scale of the problem of changing demand identified in Figure 3.4, a number of areas in the North East, Merseyside, West Midlands, West Yorkshire and the East and West Midlands required some market restructuring to address potential weakening of demand, but were outside the established Pathfinder boundaries. The final boundaries were therefore subject to a degree of negotiation between local authorities and the ODPM's Market Renewal team. Inevitably, these negotiations would have had to account for local political priorities and sensitivities, although the exact process of negotiation and decision was somewhat opaque. Indeed, there was at the time, some surprise that Teesside was not designated as a Pathfinder, given the clear scale of housing market problems there. We return to consider some of these political aspects in detail in Chapter 4 where we examine the politics and coalition building associated with HMR.

It is important to again reiterate that not all dwellings that were identified in the 'risk' areas themselves experienced low demand. Local demand factors need to be taken into account and local administrative data used to understand what is happening in neighbourhoods. Regional analyses of the type reported here need to provide a framework for a more nuanced analysis of local housing markets, including 'traditional' estimates of housing need. As a starting point for Strategic Housing Market Assessments (SHMAs), required by PPS 3 (CLG, 2006a), the risk analysis described above could be supplemented usefully by local and sub-regional data, to understand the degree of risk in neighbourhoods identified using the techniques described previously.

One of the significant local factors of concern in relation to the functioning of housing markets is the presence of a significant BME population. The original research evidence into low demand supported the suggestion that areas with significant BME populations were less likely to have generic low-demand problems, despite their tendency to exhibit high levels of deprivation. Figure 3.5 shows the distribution of all BME households in England, highlighting local authorities in the North and Midlands where the most concentrated patterns of risk emerge (those local authorities identified in Table 3.1).

It is clear that in some 'high risk' local authority areas, the concentration of BME households was (and remains) very pronounced. This was most notably the case in the Urban Living Pathfinder (Birmingham and Sandwell) where, in 2001, around 65 per cent of the population was from a BME group (Urban Living, 2006). Conversely, in other Pathfinder areas (notably NewHeartlands, Gateway and Bridging NewcastleGateshead) the concentration is far below the national average. The risk of low demand in areas with lower BME populations is heightened because the search and behaviour patterns of BME households, many of which are younger, tended to support property and neighbourhood types where the demand had otherwise declined. However, these processes operate at the local neighbourhood rather than the

Figure 3.5: Concentration of BME population (as at 1991 census) in local authorities with the highest risk of changing demand

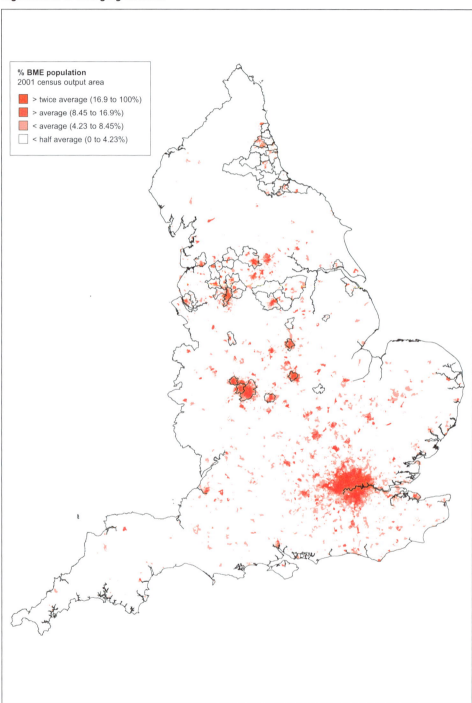

Source: authors' new analysis of CURS risk index.

metropolitan housing market level. Hence, there is evidence of low demand for social housing in some local authorities where there is a large BME population that is highly segregated, such as in Birmingham, because demand from these communities will not consider social housing in peripheral social housing estates, or living in other environments dominated by the majority non-BME population, in part due to fears of harassment (Bains, 2006; Cole and Ferrari, 2007). This again emphasises the importance of a detailed understanding of local housing market pressures.

Local housing market case studies

What is clear from the analysis of changing demand is that there are local factors (such as the demand expressed by BME households) that will mitigate the impact of changing demand on neighbourhoods. In this section, we provide four examples of how partnerships involving local housing providers and agencies developed different ways of understanding the function and trajectory of neighbourhoods, using small-area data to model low and changing demand. These are:

- Identifying the point at which vacant housing increases (developing 'tipping-point' thresholds) in Liverpool.
- Identifying housing demand 'segments' in Coventry.
- Identifying low-demand housing association housing areas in Birmingham/ Solihull.
- Modelling 'sustainable housing markets' in Birmingham.

Low demand in Liverpool

In Liverpool, a four-fold typology was used to guide the targeting of areas with the greatest risk of housing market failure in the inner core of Liverpool (see Lee and Nevin, 2002):

- Acute areas with vacancy rates and turnover rates above the hypothetical 'tipping' points of 14.5 and 16 per cent respectively.
- Acute areas with low inflow and outflow: areas with high vacancy rates, but below the 'tipping' point turnover rate.
- Areas with high turnover, but lower than 'tipping' point vacancy rates.
- Areas with below the 'tipping' point on both measures.

The areas identified are shown in Figure 3.6. The analysis identified neighbourhoods containing more than 18,000 dwellings where the average void rate varied between 25 and 30 per cent. Analysis of tenure indicated that in the most problematic 'acute core' around 40 per cent of properties were owned by housing associations.
A subsequent research process involved the use of adjacency analysis (see Appendix 3), which was then related to existing policy frameworks and additional local data in Liverpool to understand the local market context. The geographical analysis was used in the development of policy zones for Liverpool and informed the city's investment and regeneration strategy.

Figure 3.6: Typology of risk areas in Liverpool's inner core

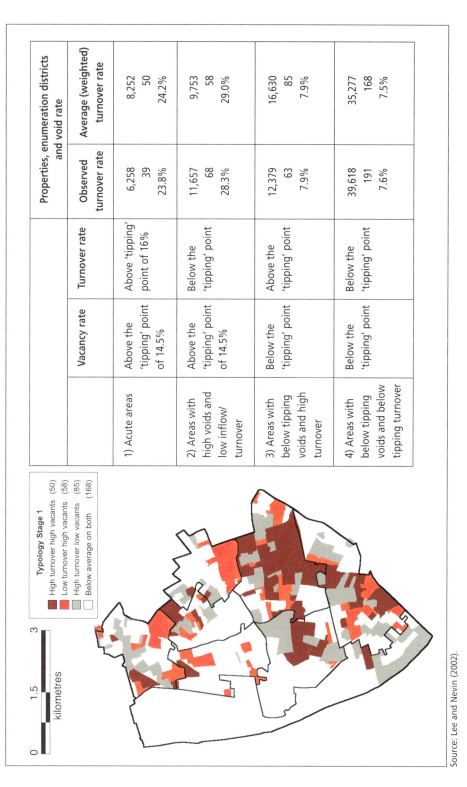

	Vacancy rate	Turnover rate	Properties, enumeration districts and void rate	
			Observed turnover rate	Average (weighted) turnover rate
1) Acute areas	Above the 'tipping' point of 14.5%	Above 'tipping' point of 16%	6,258 39 23.8%	8,252 50 24.2%
2) Areas with high voids and low inflow/ turnover	Above the 'tipping' point of 14.5%	Below the 'tipping' point	11,657 68 28.3%	9,753 58 29.0%
3) Areas with below tipping voids and high turnover	Below the 'tipping' point	Above the 'tipping' point	12,379 63 7.9%	16,630 85 7.9%
4) Areas with below tipping voids and below tipping turnover	Below the 'tipping' point	Below the 'tipping' point	39,618 191 7.6%	35,277 168 7.5%

Typology Stage 1
- High turnover high vacants (50)
- Low turnover high vacants (58)
- High turnover low vacants (85)
- Below average on both (168)

Source: Lee and Nevin (2002).

Housing 'segments' in Coventry

In Coventry, a slightly different approach was adopted. In response to concerns about the ongoing sustainability of housing markets at the neighbourhood level, there was an interest in developing a deeper understanding of the roles and functions of different parts of the local housing market.

Consequently, in what can be seen as a development of the 'at risk' approach, analysis focused on five variables at neighbourhood level with characteristics that describe the underlying 'function' of neighbourhoods within the city (Lee and Ferrari, 2005). These variables related to:

- **The very young:** the proportion of the population aged 0 to 4, a proxy for households and families possibly at the 'start' of their housing career (Primary Care Trust data).
- **The young, economically active population:** people aged 25-34, who are arguably more mobile, and on the whole, may have more flexibility in the housing choices that they can make.
- **The very old:** the proportion of households with all residents aged 75 years and over – reflecting households towards the end of their housing career.
- **Ethnicity:** recognising that housing 'preferences' sometimes lead to neighbourhoods displaying signs of segregation along ethnic lines.
- **The balance between houses and flats.**

Figure 3.7: Housing market segments in Coventry

Source: Lee and Ferrari (2005).

A simple cluster analysis was developed that was used to describe the different functions of these housing market segments (as identified in Figure 3.7). Further analysis looked at how these segments related to the wider sub-region and how they related to indicators of market outcomes (e.g. prices). The analysis played an important part in developing the investment strategy of a stock transfer housing association in Coventry.

Changing demand for housing association properties in Birmingham and Solihull

In a study of housing market demand in Birmingham-Solihull, data on new tenancies from the then Housing Corporation's Continuous Recording (CORE) data, (now collected by the Tenant Services Authority, or TSA), was geocoded and mapped at postcode level to analyse indicators of low and changing demand, and identify parts of the Birmingham/Solihull 'Eastern Corridor' regeneration area where the demand sustainability of the housing associations' stock was being undermined. Neighbourhood level analysis of lettings for the period 1998-2002 highlighted areas with the following characteristics (see Lee *et al.*, 2003a):

- Rates of lettings resulting from abandonment by the previous tenant above the national average rate (>8.2 per cent).
- Offer-to-let ratios that were above the national average (>15.6 per cent).
- Vacancy rate above national average (>21.7 per cent of lettings vacant for longer than 49 days).
- Turnover above the level then specified in best practice (DETR, 2000a) (above 13 per cent gross relets).

Clusters of areas were differentiated between areas with the following combination of circumstances:

- Highly transient areas: high abandonment (>8.2 per cent), and high turnover (>13 per cent).
- Low turnover with weakening demand: high vacancy days (>21.7 per cent or lettings previously vacant for 49 days or more), or difficult-to-let (>15.6 per cent 2 or more offers to let), and turnover low (<=13 per cent).
- High turnover areas: areas not included above, but where turnover is high (>13 per cent).
- Low turnover areas: areas not included above, but where turnover is low (<=13 per cent).

The results of this analysis are shown in Figure 3.8. There is a clear east-west distinction between areas, showing evidence suggestive of a more transient population liable to abandon properties, areas with weakening demand and low

Figure 3.8: Changing demand for housing association properties in the Birmingham/Solihull Eastern Corridor, 1998-2002

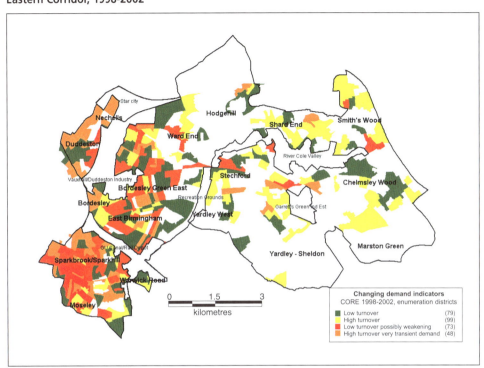

Source: Housing Corporation, CORE data 1998-2002; matched to enumeration districts.

turnover in the west of the Corridor. The analysis was developed further to produce a number of policy zones based on these characteristics and on the directions of change or trajectories of areas.

Sustainable housing markets in Birmingham

During the period 2003-2004, Birmingham City Council's housing department developed a 'Sustainable Housing Markets Index' (SHMI). The development of the index arose from a series of corporate level meetings within the city council at which senior officers from different policy areas (e.g., housing, planning, economic development and environmental services), agreed to develop a shared analysis of the 'state of the city'. Cross-departmental indicators relating to educational attainment, housing demand and condition, crime levels and transport connectivity were generated at the smallest spatial scale available (postcode/output area) and overlaid onto a map of the city's 'Housing Market Areas' (HMAs). The indicators chosen recognised the multifaceted nature of community 'sustainability' and reflected the approach advocated by the Egan review of skills for sustainable communities (Figure 3.9).

Figure 3.9: The Egan 'wheel' of sustainable communities

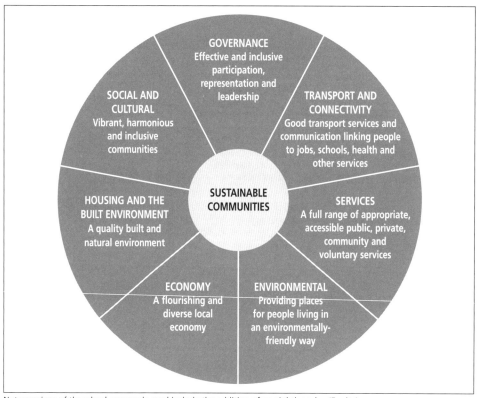

Note: versions of the wheel commonly used include the addition of an eighth spoke: 'Equity'.
Source: Egan Review (2004).

The city council had invested in the development of GIS to visualise aspects of housing market change and had developed an agreed set of Housing Market Area (HMA) boundaries based on house prices, housing demand and migration: the Birmingham HMA boundaries shown at Figure 3.10 are contiguous zones that cut across administrative ward boundaries. The sustainability index was intended to be an ongoing monitoring tool and centre-piece of the city's housing strategy (BCC, 2005). Furthermore, the HMAs were used to report the results of residents' satisfaction surveys, housing aspiration surveys, housing needs surveys and analysis of Decent Homes investment.

An innovative feature of the SHMI project was that it used data from a variety of sources, including the aforementioned surveys, to cross-check the analysis of secondary data sets. For example, a housing aspirations/intentions survey carried out in 2003 was used to validate and support spatial analysis from the sustainability index. In another example, the sustainability index was updated using weights from the residents' intention/aspiration survey to provide a more 'realistic' set of housing market drivers, that reflected residents' and households' housing market behaviour, specifically relating to their perceptions about crime levels.

Figure 3.11: Sustainable Housing Markets in Birmingham

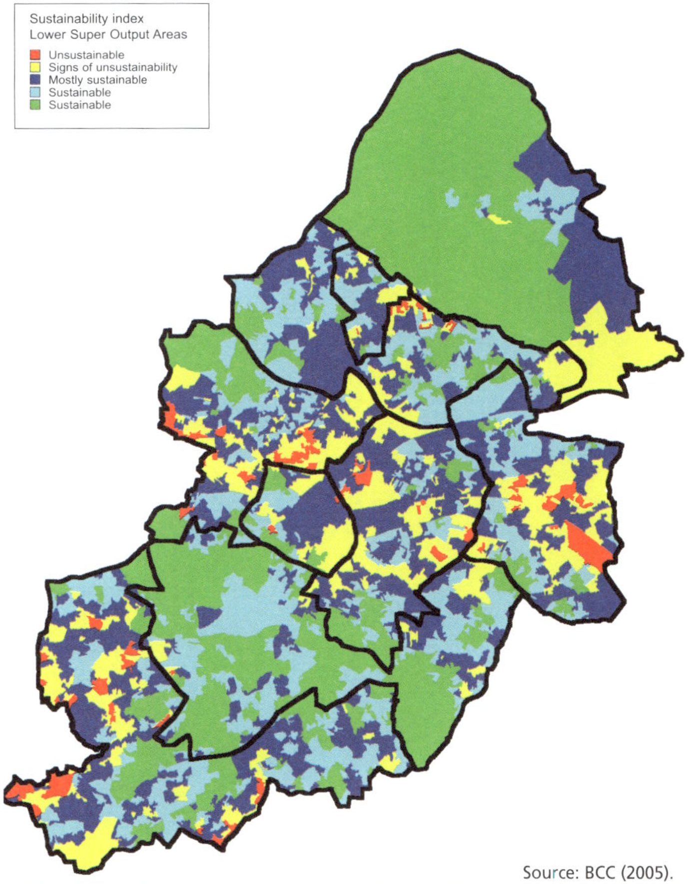

Source: BCC (2005).

Sustainability index
Lower Super Output Areas
- Unsustainable
- Signs of unsustainability
- Mostly sustainable
- Sustainable
- Sustainable

Figure 3.10: Birmingham's Housing Market Areas

Source: BCC (2005).

Housing Market Areas
- City Centre
- East Birmingham
- Eastern Periphery
- North West Birmingham
- Northern Periphery
- Northern Suburbs
- Southern Periphery
- Suburban Ring North
- Suburban Ring South

Ward boundaries
- Ward name

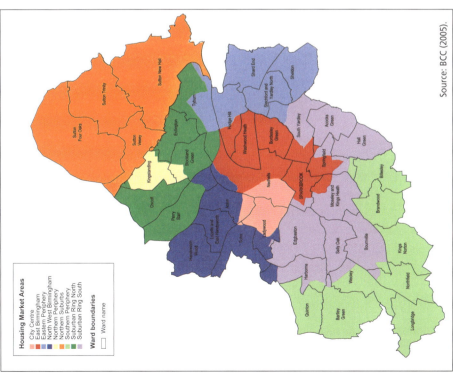

Results from the 2004 sustainability index are shown in Figure 3.11. Areas shaded green to blue were considered relatively 'healthy'; areas shaded yellow were considered to be on the 'cusp' and showing signs of 'tipping' into more problematic levels of unsustainability; areas shaded red were considered to be exhibiting distinct signs of unsustainability with concerns about the levels of crime, housing demand and access to services and jobs. The analysis was used to highlight areas of the city for intervention and to cross-reference with strategic investments such as the Decent Homes programme.

Approaches such as that described here contributed to the city council being commended on its innovative use of GIS and strategic housing intelligence by the Audit Commission (2009). The advances in analysis have been matched by the development of a new architecture for policy development in housing and regeneration, in itself partly in response to the creation of the Homes and Communities Agency (HCA), and its 'single conversation' approach to investment. In Birmingham, Housing Investment Groups (HIGs), have been established for each Housing Market Area with chairpersons nominated from the RDA (Advantage West Midlands), the HCA and representatives from the city's housing and planning departments. The development of innovative intelligence systems, and an inclusive strategic management structure, provides a secure footing for developing resilient and sustainable housing markets in the future. The importance of interpreting analysis within an appropriate strategic and policy infrastructure is highlighted by the Birmingham example. Another good example in this vein, is Bridging NewcastleGateshead's 'Vitality Index', which is the subject of regular reports to the Pathfinder's strategic board. The close integration of evidence and strategic decision-making is one of the 'three Ds' of good market intelligence advocated by Robinson *et al.* (2005).

Summary

In this chapter we have brought together for the first time the various methods used in developing the evidence base for assessing the risk of low and changing demand. Although arguments have been made subsequently about the appropriateness and timeliness of data and methods used in these models, there were clearly some innovations and they demonstrated a comprehensive local commitment to developing genuine 'evidence-based policy'. Cross-boundary working, extensive consultation on detailed small areas statistics and use of the census of population in a way that had not been used before, brought together both 'top down' and 'bottom up' approaches. Local authority officers were aware of problems with the demand for housing in many neighbourhoods well before the academic models described in this chapter were able to quantify them. While the evidence base for HMR has been criticised as being merely a technical exercise, such criticism ignores the real inputs of local officers and the frequent use of more qualitative methods in understanding local housing markets. Whatever its shortcomings, we would consider the work of local authorities at the time to be a real attempt to apply contemporary conceptualisations about mobility, the market and spatial dynamics for local housing and neighbourhood policy-making.

The sub-regional analyses of 'risk' developed by CURS, were accompanied by a range of local studies by local authorities assessing the exposure of local markets and neighbourhoods to low and changing demand. The evidence indicated, for example, that housing associations were over-exposed to weakening demand in parts of the North and Midlands, where the housing market function of neighbourhoods had changed. Although around two million people, living in more than 800,000 houses, are covered by HMR Pathfinders in England, it is also clear that there were areas with significant housing market problems outside the areas that were eventually designated as Pathfinders. Referring back to our comments in the opening chapter, we include here those areas where 'high end' market failure has occurred and where affordability and community mix problems have arisen.

The development of these regional, sub-regional and local analyses of the housing market influenced the nature and content of the Pathfinders prospectuses, as we will see in Chapter 4. A broader appreciation of market dynamics also underpinned the subsequent development of Strategic Housing Market Assessments (SHMAs) (see Jones and Watkins, 2009). The analyses featured in this chapter signalled a need for policy-makers and housing providers to monitor changes for investment purposes, paying particular attention to:

- The sub-regional and regional context of changing demand.
- Spatial analyses incorporating 'adjacency analysis' and the 'coalescence' of risk (adjacency analysis of the spatial coalescence of risk factors in order to understand the pattern of low and changing demand), in order to put into context the spatial patterns of low and changing demand (see Appendix 3 for details of the 'adjacency analysis' method).
- Contextualising local factors such as the segregated patterns of BME communities, future aspirations and mapping of locally held administrative data.
- Utilising local and regional/sub-regional data in a way that throws light on the trajectory and function of neighbourhoods, and not just 'static' measures of disadvantage and social-economic needs.
- The identification of housing market segments and housing sub-markets and their associated trajectories.

CHAPTER 4:
Developing local approaches to market renewal

Introduction

This chapter considers how analysis of low and changing demand for housing was translated into a programme of action for local housing markets. Although Housing Market Renewal was announced by Whitehall as a regeneration programme within the national Sustainable Communities Plan, the analysis of the issues and the implications for the response remained inherently local or sub-regional. The importance of developing a flexible local response to a detailed understanding of local issues within the structure of a national policy, lies at the heart of the HMR approach, and explains some of its tensions. Of particular relevance is an understanding of the political context for intervention.

This chapter begins by considering the importance of local political coalition building for the genesis of HMR and shaping the possibilities of local responses. It then goes on to consider the development of renewal strategies at the Pathfinder level. It does so through the lens of case studies of selected Pathfinder 'prospectuses' – their strategic plans agreed with government – and the connection between their strategic objectives and the needs implied by regional and local analyses of housing markets.

Local coalition building: the politics of Housing Market Renewal (HMR)

In March 2002, the final report of the Select Committee enquiry into empty homes (HC 240-I, 2001-02) made strong calls for a market renewal strategy. By the next month, the nine Housing Market Renewal (HMR) Pathfinders had been announced and a pump-priming resource of £24 million had been made available from the Capital Modernisation Fund for their initial work. As a government policy, Housing Market Renewal had, therefore, quite a rapid genesis. The speed with which a concern with housing market problems in northern cities, articulated through local coalition building and evidence gathering, prompted the formation of dedicated agencies of response, was in some respects astonishing. There were a number of explanations for the rapid rise of low and changing demand for housing in the political consciousness of the government and the formulations of a set of policy goals within the Sustainable Communities Plan. These included:

- **Reconciliation of both spatial and social exclusion:** HMR provided one housing market-led solution to help spatial planning policy reduce the mismatch between communities and the opportunities arising in the local and regional economy.
- **Political backing:** It was championed by 'heavyweight' labour grandees John Prescott, Stephen Byers (as head of DTLR when the Sustainable Communities Plan was announced) and Lord Falconer, who together gave the concept its political traction. Lord Falconer as housing, planning and regeneration minister, played a significant role in the establishment of Housing Market Renewal Pathfinders. Prescott was indispensable to New Labour, as he was seen to understand the northern localities that were home to many working-class Labour supporters (Ashley, 2001). In much the same way, he was indispensable to the HMR project, which offered something to the Labour heartlands. As deputy prime minister and, at the time, the lead politician in the Cabinet Office, he occupied a pivotal role in co-ordinating the different strands of policy, and understood the importance of market renewal to the Sustainable Communities Plan.
- **Local coalitions:** There was momentum and pressure generated by the 'low and changing demand' coalition, which funded the original 'M62 Corridor' report by CURS (see Figure 4.1). The consortium included leading figures in the social housing 'industry', such as Max Steinberg and Jim Battle (then at the Housing Corporation and National Housing Federation respectively), and was organised by Brendan Nevin, whose ability to reconcile the academic evidence base with the politics of the moment, led to his identification by the *Guardian* as one of the UK's leading public policy figures (*Society Guardian*, 2003). The coalition raised the profile of the low-demand problem in the North West and brought it to the attention of senior civil servants and politicians.

These were important features that underpinned the development and success of realising the evidence into firm action and commitment by government. The rapid crystallisation of HMR as a policy tool meant that the detail on local strategy and policy intervention was to be formulated by the Pathfinders themselves in the year following the announcement of the Sustainable Communities Plan. No precise template for this was provided. Pathfinders were tasked with developing prospectuses outlining their evidence base and proposed intervention programme for the period to 2006. In 2002 and early 2003, each of the Pathfinders set down the road of visioning how HMR would work in their area. It was in these prospectuses (and the strategic thinking that went into their preparation), that local innovations in understanding the market and the fruits of the vast market renewal evidence base that was already well established, were expected to pay dividends. Many of the arguments of ideology and principal had already been won, as the intense period of debate and research into low demand and the rapid policy genesis lies in testament. It was then up to each of the Pathfinders to translate a national strategy and idea into something tangible, meaningful and deliverable at the local level.

Figure 4.1: How the housing press reported on the bid to the Comprehensive Spending Review for a market renewal fund

HOUSING*today*

www.housingtoday.org.uk   8 November 2001 **Issue 259**

NOISE ANNOYS: Weymouth and Portland mayor Joy Stanley last week drove a Chieftain tank over a pile of stereos and TVs to highlight the neighbourhood nuisance problems caused by loud music.

All the flattened items had been seized by the council's environmental health department in the past two years.

Noise problems caused by loud music were on the increase, environmental health officer Tony Beason said.

West Midlands and north councils and RSLs petition government as market collapse continues

Regions seek rebuild millions

by Janis Bright
j.bright@easynet.co.uk

A unique grouping of landlords, councils and representative organisations in northern England and the west Midlands is preparing a mammoth bid for government funding to renew housing in areas where markets are collapsing, *Housing Today* has learned.

The bid to establish a special market renewal fund in next year's comprehensive spending review is certain to run to hundreds of millions of pounds, and into billions longer-term. It is backed by evidence from the groundbreaking Birmingham university studies of housing markets in the M62 corridor and west Midlands, released earlier this year.

The submission, first floated at a meeting in September with junior housing minister Sally Keeble, will include costed examples of possible remedies from three sample areas.

The grouping includes the three northern housing forums, the National Housing Federation, the key cities group including Birmingham, and the Northern Consortium of Housing Authorities.

The research, by the university's Centre for Urban and Regional Studies, caused alarm in the sector when it revealed the extent of market collapse (*Housing Today*, 8 February, and 17 May).

The M62 report found 280,000 homes in areas "at risk" and developed a model for pinpointing housing types and areas most likely to suffer abandonment.

The west Midlands research highlighted decades of "white flight" with black and minority ethnic communities left trapped in inner areas of poor housing. Parallel research is underway in the north east and in Yorkshire and Humberside.

North West Housing Forum link officer Steven Fyfe said that the aim was to establish a government commitment for 15 to 20 years. "This exercise is about returning value to areas that otherwise will not have a tremendous future," he told *Housing Today*. "That means attracting the private sector and individuals back to them. But markets need certainty. Councils will have to give long term commitments on any interventions."

The amount of government support needed has proved difficult to quantify because some areas already have programmes running. "The do-nothing option has costs too," he warned.

The group wants to see action on a far greater scale than current programmes such as the Neighbourhood Renewal Fund. One option is to form new organisations to channel all programmes into a single pot, similar to the old urban development corporations.

Fyfe added: "There will obviously need to be structures. But at present outcomes are much more important."

National Housing Federation head of northern regions Jim Battle added: "This is a key piece of work in establishing what policy initiatives are needed."

Source: *Housing Today*, 8 November 2001.

It should have come as no surprise that this was unlikely to have ever been an easy task. That the housing market was no respecter of administrative geography was an idea well accepted by local government. But, the practice of cross-boundary working remained relatively untested on the ground. At the same time, Pathfinders were expected to respond to a multiplicity of different drivers of change in what was really quite a heterogeneous set of circumstances. The physical symptoms of low demand may have been the same in Barnsley as they were in Bootle, but the drivers and spatial configurations of the local market in these areas – despite sharing some structural commonalities – were very different.

The scale of HMR as a form of regeneration policy was beyond that previously imagined. As is evident from Table 4.1, most of the Pathfinder's intervention areas are the size of small cities in their own right. This size brought with it a level of complexity in terms of the issues at stake and the political representation that was beyond that of other regeneration policies. Despite the fact that government selected the intervention areas, there was a palpable sense of competition emerging between Pathfinders as, through their prospectuses, they were, in effect, bidding for a share of the initial £500 million HMR pie. While not exactly a race, the kudos of completing a prospectus and submitting it for ministerial approval earlier than the others was quite clearly a goal that was perceived to be worth attaining. That the Manchester-Salford Partnership (MSP) was by some margin the first to submit its prospectus and was quickly allocated £125 million (a quarter of the national budget for the programme), doubtless cemented the importance of 'not coming last' in the minds of the remaining eight.

Table 4.1: Basic characteristics of the HMR Pathfinders

Pathfinder	Area (hectares)	Population		Households	
		2001 (persons)	Change since 1991 (%)	2001 (number)	Change since 1991 (%)
Urban Living	3,295	152,354	- 5.5	57,160	- 1.5
Renew North Staffordshire	5,612	146,637	- 2.5	64,100	4.3
NewHeartlands	5,402	246,464	- 9.6	109,647	- 4.1
Manchester-Salford Partnership	6,379	240,370	- 7.9	102,085	- 7.0
Partners in Action	4,946	183,143	- 0.2	72,593	0.2
Elevate East Lancashire	8,818	206,770	- 3.3	81,754	- 1.5
Transform South Yorkshire	14,286	297,887	- 4.4	125,132	- 1.1
Gateway	6,847	241,412	- 4.8	103,078	0.0
Bridging NewcastleGateshead	3,686	154,790	- 9.3	68,716	- 6.1
All Pathfinders	59,271	1,869,827	- 5.5	784,265	- 2.2

Source: Leather *et al.* (2007, p.15).

HMR prospectuses: the evidence and drivers

In the rest of this chapter we take a closer look at how the Pathfinders were able to set about formulating their own distinctive local approaches to market renewal. The government's emphasis for the programme had always been on innovation and it was clear from the outset that local solutions needed to be designed and delivered for a variety of different markets and contexts. The real innovation in HMR was expected to come at the local level – yet, at the same time, it was arguably a policy whose existence was determined in a very top down fashion. The lack, for instance, of a competitive element to the selection of areas appeared to break with the sort of approach to urban regeneration policy that City Challenge and Single Regeneration Budget had come to epitomise.

The Pathfinders all identified a range of housing market 'drivers' and either used in-house research and analysis to inform their prospectus, or otherwise commissioned external consultants to develop 'holistic' accounts of the local housing market. Such 'holistic' accounts meant different things in different places and the Pathfinders' prospectuses reflected a plurality of approaches. In its advocacy of HMR, the 2002 Select Committee report stressed that:

> *Different solutions are required in different places, taking account of the circumstances facing the housing market in each conurbation and the need to manage change. The rules governing a Housing Market Renewal Fund must provide sufficient flexibility to take account of that diversity* (HC 240-I, 2001-02, para. 155).

A number of the Pathfinders provided comprehensive statistical appendices and bespoke research reports to underpin their evidence base and justify their proposed interventions. The Merseyside Pathfinder 'NewHeartlands' was typical in this respect, drawing on a range of bespoke and existing evidence to provide an overarching commentary and analysis of market weakness and opportunities. Hence, such studies as the Merseyside Urban Housing Capacity Study (2003); CURS' analysis of the Liverpool housing market (1999-2003); the Merseyside Economic Review; the Merseyside Urban Housing Capacity Study (2003); Merseyside Housing Demand Study (2003); CURS' Changing Housing Markets and Urban Regeneration in the M62 Corridor Study (2000), and Sefton Council's Private Sector Stock Condition Survey (2003), all formed part of the significant evidence base for the NewHeartlands prospectus. Other Pathfinders compiled comparable evidence bases. The range of concerns is reflected in the Pathfinders' approaches and can be seen in the themes that their prospectuses address. We have considered the prospectuses for the nine original Pathfinders according to the following themes as well as the methods used to address these themes:

- the economy;
- house prices;

- residents' perceptions (from both within and outside Pathfinder areas);
- housing 'stress';
- vacant property;
- crime;
- demography;
- migration; and
- labour market connections.

The development by the Pathfinders of neighbourhood-based models, especially where these focus on neighbourhood 'function' and change is also considered. These holistic accounts of the local housing market, across tenures and emphasising the importance of sub-markets, presaged the way that subsequent housing market guidance (CLG, 2007b) would consider the analysis of housing markets in Strategic Housing Market Assessments (SHMAs). The Pathfinders' neighbourhood-based models provided an opportunity to take stock of how the housing market worked as a wider system (Gibney *et al.*, 2009), and how 'joined-up' thinking and cross-boundary working for the purpose of delivering resilient and sustainable housing markets was developed.

The economy as a housing market driver

The role of the economy and its future trajectory were clearly influential factors with implications for the level and type of demand for housing. Table 4.2 demonstrates the importance of the economy in constructing the evidence base and drivers in the Pathfinders' prospectuses. All of the prospectuses dealt with the economy in their submissions, although the emphasis varied considerably in terms of the level of detailed analysis.

This coverage reflects the role of the economy as a significant influence within the low and changing demand debates that gave rise to HMR. The changing demand debate referred to the way in which housing in older industrial urban cores had been built to service a different economic era. HMR thus represented an opportunity and mechanism to re-calibrate the local housing market so that it fitted more effectively with the 'new urban economy'. From what we understand about the asymmetry between housing and labour markets (Allen and Hamnett, 1991) our cities and regions today are the legacy of historic development and economic agglomeration (Wannop and Cherry, 1994; Musterd, 2006), that has occurred in response to a number of economic signals and over a number of periods of development. These legacies point to a degree of path dependency of space, whereby previous policy eras (whether positive or negative), affect and shape subsequent policy eras and interventions (see Kay, 2005). Lee and Murie (2004) summarise this in the identification of four distinct phases in which the function of housing has been inextricably linked to the role of the economy:

Table 4.2: Evidence base characteristics of Pathfinders' prospectuses

Characteristic	Partners in Action	Manchester-Salford Partnership	Bridging NewcastleGateshead	Renew North Staffordshire	Elevate East Lancashire	NewHeartlands	Transform South Yorkshire	Urban Living	Gateway
Housing tenure	✓	✓	✓	✓	✓	✓	✓	✓	✓
Size of properties	✓								
Council tax bands	✓	✓		✓	✓	✓	✓	✓	✓
Type/design of housing	✓	✓	✓	✓	✓	✓	✓	✓	✓
'Connectedness' to economic opportunities	✓	✓	✓	✓		✓	✓		
Stock condition					✓	✓ (C)			✓
Vacant housing	✓ (BA)	✓	✓	✓			✓	✓	
Household turnover	✓ (S)			✓		✓ (C)	✓		✓
Ethnicity of population	✓		✓	✓		✓	✓		
House prices	✓ (RA, PT)	✓	✓	✓	✓	✓	✓	✓	✓
Multiple deprivation	✓ (IMD)	✓ (IMD)	✓ (IMD)	✓ (IMD)	✓ (IMD)	✓ (C)	✓ (IMD)	✓	✓
Social deprivation & family breakdown		✓							
Household income	✓ (BS)			✓	✓ (IS)	✓ (C)	✓		
Health		✓					✓	✓ (C)	
Demographics	✓	✓	✓	✓		✓ (C)	✓	✓ (C)	
Migration/population mobility			✓			✓ (C)			
Neighbourhood satisfaction	✓ (BS)			✓		✓ (C)			
Housing aspirations	✓ (BS)							✓	
Local economy	✓	✓	✓	✓	✓	✓	✓	✓	✓
Skills	✓	✓			✓				
Crime & community safety	✓	✓	✓	✓		✓ (C)	✓	✓	✓
Environmental quality	✓ (C)	✓		✓				✓	
Local facilities/transport	✓ (C)							✓	✓
Education	✓ (BA)	✓	✓ (BA)	✓		✓ (C)	✓		

RA: comparison to regional average; S: social housing turnover only; IS: income support and benefit dependency; PT: comparison of property types; BA: comparison to borough/district average; BS: bespoke survey; C: commentary only – no data sources given.

- **Production of primary manufacturing and raw materials:** In this phase, working-class housing developed in these places to bring workers to the workplace (see Wannop and Cherry, 1994).
- **Increased productivity and personal mobility:** The development of personal mobility, and in particular the motor car, meant that the skilled artisan class was no longer confined to living in walking distance of the place of employment.
- **The maturation of housing markets:** In this phase, changes in the role of the economy to more service-led spheres resulted in a separation of housing and economic functions. The location of services was not strictly determined by the location of production of housing, therefore the older housing no longer fitted with the original economic function.
- **Housing as an investment:** The increased affluence of households and the aspiration for home ownership led to a situation in which the life plans of many households included a significant investment in housing (Lee and Murie, 2004, pp.236-238). This has only recently been challenged by the 'sub-prime' market collapse associated with the most recent economic downturn.

The argument therefore proceeded that whilst developed economies had diversified, some of the housing stock had not kept pace with these developments. The spatial consequences were that housing which had been built with a primary or manufacturing function became increasingly unattractive to new households. In Newcastle upon Tyne, for example, 'housing choice' was the major reason cited for households migrating to the surrounding sub-region and for jobs leaving the region:

> *The Tyneside flat built pre-1919 was appropriate to a riverside manufacturing area, but may not meet decency and aspiration levels of current residents or attract new ones* (Bridging NewcastleGateshead, 2003, p.10).

The argument for HMR intervention was built on the premise that, in some areas, a more flexible global economy, demanding more footloose labour, was increasingly adrift from the fixed and immobile housing stock. Whilst flows of financial capital became ever more flexible, production techniques such as 'just-in-time' methods, the rise of niche marketing and the commodification of information, meant that the global economy could deliver 'flexible specialisation', a departure from the patterns of mass consumption and production associated with the Fordist era (Amin, 1994). Housing could not respond in the same way. Housing's answer to flexible specialisation has been, and will continue to be, the reinvention of housing forms and neighbourhoods to perform a different function, or, cater for a new set of social or economic needs. Although there are specific examples such as the 'studentification' of inner city areas of terrace housing (Smith, 2008), or the recycling of unpopular seaside accommodation for the housing of homeless people, the theory of 'filtering' has long held that, because of the immobility of housing, the hierarchical position of housing and the neighbourhoods it occupies will inevitably change (see Galster, 1996, for a review).

Within the spirit of this logic, the prospectuses proceeded to build up a core narrative that demonstrated and evaluated the extent of the asymmetry between local housing markets and labour markets and the extent to which intervention might be needed to re-calibrate these two divergent 'systems'. The emphasis was conceived and debated in the context of the changing economic fortunes in, and the improved housing offer on the edge of, conurbations which was being reflected in the long-term fall in male unemployment and a decline in the absolute numbers on council housing waiting lists, as evidenced in the highly influential M62 Corridor report (Figure 4.2). This evidence was subsequently used to support the restructuring of housing markets:

> *CURS concluded that 'neighbourhoods at risk (of changing demand) are predominantly social housing areas'. Their analysis also demonstrated 'an almost perfect statistical relationship between fall in male unemployment and the fall in waiting lists for social housing 1992-99'. Their main recommendation was a 'strategic restructuring of housing markets* (House of Commons, 2008, p.41).

Figure 4.2: The relationship between male unemployment and waiting lists (standardised 'z scores', 1992-1999)

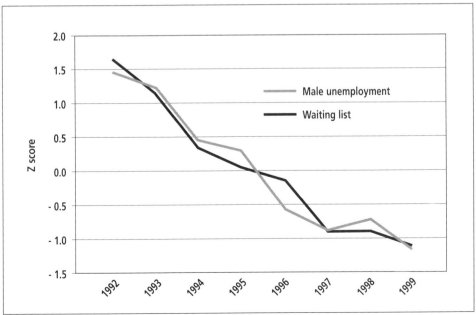

Source: Nevin, Lee *et al.* (2000).

The second element in this debate concerned the proactive role that housing could play in stimulating the economy. The argument proceeded that the housing 'offer' needed to be sufficiently diverse in terms of the range and type of housing available in order to attract and/or retain a diversity of households at different life stages and with varying incomes. A monolithic offer, or one with no housing opportunities for higher-income groups, would diminish the prospect and potential for diversifying households and increasing the tax base of the local authority. If there are no housing opportunities for higher-income groups then the potential for diversifying both the housing offer and increasing the tax base of the local authority is reduced. As the economy changed, the housing and neighbourhood offer declined as a result of this. Reinvigorating the economy through a combined assault on housing and the economy was perhaps a lost opportunity when the urban development corporations were set up in the 1980s. The UDCs in many areas focused on transforming the economic uses of land and brought about only limited benefits to local residential neighbourhoods, partly because new workers were drawn from wider areas (Syrett and North, 2008, pp.167-8). Burfitt and Ferrari (2008) predicted a similar effect for more contemporary 'high tech' economic developments in Birmingham on the basis of a lack of fit between housing and economic development strategies. Housing Market Renewal was therefore in some ways the (belated) response to a perceived need for a proactive intervention in the housing market and to address the asymmetry between local housing and labour markets.

In this vein, the Bridging NewcastleGateshead prospectus (Figure 4.3) drew links between changes in the local economy, the loss of traditional manufacturing employment, a process of population out-migration to take up new employment, and the increasingly polarised age structure of the residual population in part of the Pathfinder's area. The lack of diversity in the housing market, they argued, had resulted in a high proportion of employees commuting into the Pathfinder to work for larger employers in the area, such as Sanofi Winthrop and Nestlé. The Renew North Staffordshire prospectus (Figure 4.3) provided a separate annex on the housing market implications of economic change and made considerable effort to compare the performance and size of its central business district (CBD) to comparable city centres such as Leicester and Nottingham.

The prospectuses demonstrated a considerable evidence base in relation to the economy and how the housing market within their areas had been by-passed, or, had developed asymmetrically alongside their emerging sub-regional and regional economies. HMR was therefore viewed as a tool for re-calibrating the (re)development of local housing and local economy.

In the introductory chapter we noted how the 'social exclusion' agenda, became replaced by a competitiveness agenda, which embraced housing by asking, 'how does housing fit within the competitive economy?'. It is clear from the HMR prospectuses that the policy 'mindset' was part of this overarching process of finding,

Figure 4.3: Bridging NewcastleGateshead (BNG) (2003) and Renew North Staffordshire prospectuses (March 2004)

or reimagining, housing's position within a narrative of economic competitiveness. In the following chapter, we argue that this emphasis on the economy 'crowded out' other perspectives, and contributed to a backlash from local communities to the Pathfinder's plans. We also return later to the implications of an over-elaboration of economic drivers in connection to the current credit crisis in the conclusion.

House prices

The HMR programme was given the principle objective of raising house prices, so that the gap between the Pathfinders and the regional average was reduced and this immediately signalled tensions in policy concerning the intended target group. But was HMR principally concerned with raising prices and the offer, so that existing residents could choose to stay? Or, was it about a fundamental change in the symbolic capital of the HMR Pathfinders and an emphasis upon the attraction of higher-income groups from outside the Pathfinder? In some ways, this emphasis on price was to become problematic. It exposed the programme to charges that it was tantamount to an official policy of 'gentrification', where government policy was aimed specifically at eradicating low-cost housing and introducing higher-value housing. Certainly, the house price boom, when it reached Pathfinder areas, meant that questions of the affordability of housing in these areas became more important.

Notwithstanding this, 'changing demand' emphasised the cross-tenure nature of housing market weakness, and demanded that house prices signals were brought within the purview of social and urban policy. Low prices were characterised as problematic first and foremost because it indicated a lack of confidence in local housing markets. Beyond this, there was also concern that wider gaps between different quality and price levels in the housing market might hinder social and residential mobility and consequently serve to socially exclude low-income households. Such outcomes would run counter to key New Labour promises on meritocracy and the 'level playing field'. At the neighbourhood level, increasing price polarisation also undermined objectives associated with 'sustainable communities' and the mix of property and household types these objectives sought to bring about.

When the changing demand debate ignited, there had been much emphasis on the low prices realised by properties being sold in areas at risk of low demand. An emphasis on prices was one way in which the polarisation of housing markets had become evident. This was true both at the local and regional scale. There was concern that growth in house values in the South was outstripping that in the North and Midlands, and also that gaps between high-value and low-value neighbourhoods within these regions were becoming more pronounced. The extent to which prices in Pathfinder areas were falling behind regional averages became a particular focus (see for example Figure 4.4).

Figure 4.4: Tracking terrace house prices against the regional average in Oldham and Rochdale

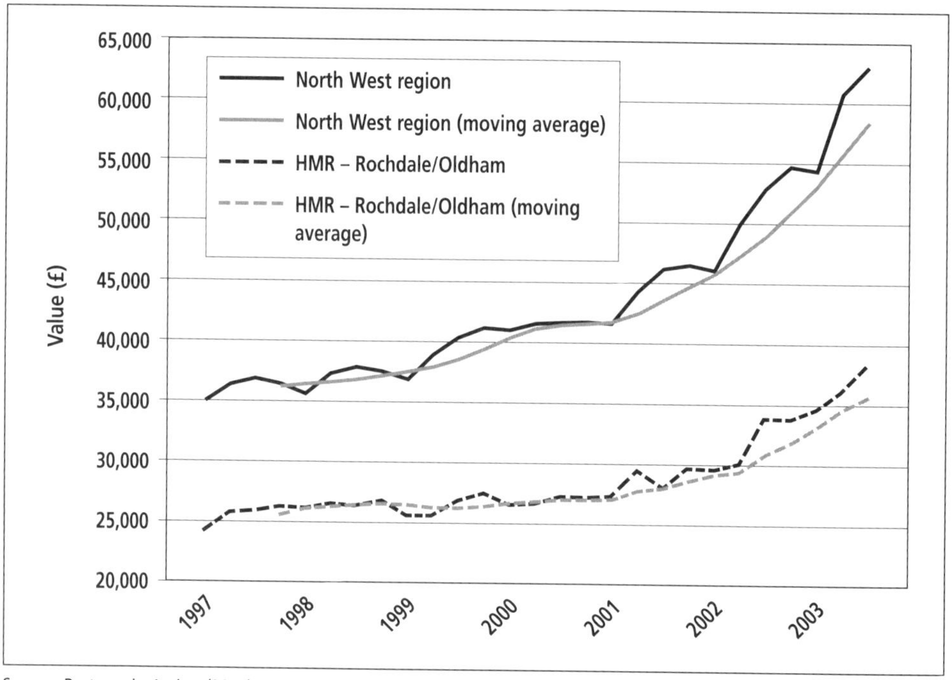

Source: Partners in Action (2003).

All of the Pathfinders analysed house price trends: firstly, mainly because the aim of Pathfinders was to reduce regional and sub-regional differences in price performance – through their interventions prices would be stabilised and increased; and secondly, because of the availability of a consistent series of house prices geocoded to a variety of spatial scales and available across England and Wales via HM Land Registry data. Urban Living provided a technical appendix to its prospectus, analysing house price change at postcode level and showing detailed comparisons of change over several years. The analysis demonstrated the segregated nature of the housing market and the growing gap between the Pathfinder and the regional average. The analysis of house prices at various spatial scales within the prospectuses reflected both the theoretical and policy thinking behind the policy – and such an objective aimed to help focus minds and attention on attracting new households with a different socio-economic profile from the existing residents.

One of the criticisms of HMR has been its insensitivity to the heritage of the built form that is represented in the terrace house. Critics such as Save Britain's Heritage (2006) point to the successful rehabilitation of terrace housing in gentrifying areas such as Islington, London. Both the critics and the original analysts, however, generally fail to fully acknowledge the diversity of the terrace housing stock. Large terrace town houses with period features set in generous streets are very different from the 'mean' terraces of brick housing, set without foundations, that so horrified George Orwell as far back as the 1930s. In retrospect, while small area statistics were widely used in modelling the risk of housing market change, more perhaps needed to be done to subject the findings to local tests of veracity through 'grounding' the evidence and triangulating a range of methods and perspectives.

Many of the prospectuses therefore provided house price analysis broken down by house type. Land Registry data on house prices allows only the most rudimentary analysis of house type i.e., detached, semi, terrace and flat; but it is through analyses of property type that the most emblematic aspects of HMR have found expression. The original CURS analysis included the proportion of terrace housing and flatted accommodation as indicators underpinning the concept of the risk of changing demand for housing. The logic here was that the immobility and durable nature of housing meant that the housing stock was unable to change in line with societal change and shifts in consumer preferences. In the parlance of HMR, terrace housing (in particular), having been speculatively provided in a former economic era, was now an 'obsolete' archetype; however, the statistics we used to understand local housing stock – principally the ten-yearly population census and the Land Registry's record of house sales – fail to make this distinction. It is therefore very difficult for local market analysis to capture these significant qualitative distinctions. Some of the prospectuses used information from stock surveys to estimate the number of older terrace properties (pre-1919), comparing the proportion of terrace housing and social housing against the borough averages (see, for example, PiA, 2003).

The explosion of information technology and availability of data at small area level was also reflected in the way that the Pathfinder made extensive use of administrative data such as council tax registers. This was used for a variety of purposes including the mapping of the number of properties in each council tax band and estimating the number of empty properties. There was a range of techniques used to estimate vacancies, but these typically would depend on various discount statuses being recorded within the register.

Given the centrality of 'turnover' and 'residential mobility' to the operation of the housing market, it is perhaps disappointing that so few of the original Pathfinder prospectuses did not contain a detailed analysis of population or housing turnover. Some Pathfinders such as Transform South Yorkshire were able to exploit well-developed social housing management systems within their local authorities, to calculate detailed measures of turnover, and the use of CORE data for housing association lettings was used to evidence difficult-to-let and abandoned properties. However, this was much more difficult to achieve across all housing tenures. The private rented sector was particularly under-represented in Pathfinders' analyses, mainly because of the difficulties in obtaining secondary data on the sector. In a pre-HMR study of housing market function, Lee and Nevin (2002) used the council tax register to impute the tenure status of 'payee' and 'statutory payee', in order to provide an impressionistic picture of the changing tenure characteristics of neighbourhoods. Some of the earliest analyses of low and changing demand emphasised high rates of turnover in being indicative of a 'loosening' of local market conditions. Keenan's (1998) study of Newcastle upon Tyne considered the frequency with which local households were able to 'churn' around local neighbourhoods. His graphical depiction of the detailed processes of turnover at a street-by-street level (Figure 4.5), powerfully demonstrated how low demand for properties could effectively empty out local housing markets and enable a more fluid, and less competitive, environment for the exchange of properties (see Keenan, 1998, p.39).

Connectedness

Measures of the proximity or connectedness of Pathfinder areas to wider economic opportunities were often used to highlight the importance of economic links to the sustainability of local housing markets. In some cases, this implied a change of function or role within regional economies, as relatively isolated, formerly economically-insulated settlements struggled to adapt to new outside pressures and a more outward-looking economy. The maturation of housing markets and the asymmetry of housing-economy elevated the importance of other drivers such as location, services and the absence of crime in determining housing market behaviour and choices, and house prices, as a measure of housing market performance, encapsulated in a number of dimensions of the house and environ which the Pathfinders attempted to reflect upon in their submissions. Some Pathfinders, for example, emphasised the proximity of valued leisure or environmental assets, underpinning a 'quality of life' agenda. Partners in Action (PiA) in Oldham-Rochdale highlighted the location of the Pennines and a good

Figure 4.5: Processes of household mobility in west Newcastle upon Tyne

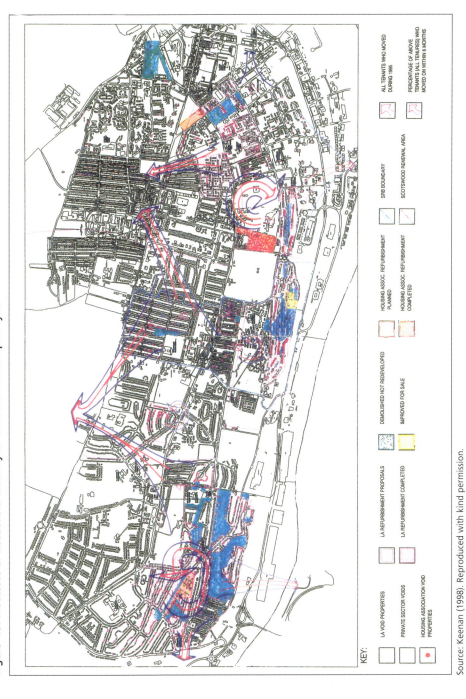

Source: Keenan (1998). Reproduced with kind permission.

environment, good access to rail links and the motorway network, and the fact that 80 per cent of the Pathfinder's housing stock was within two miles of a town centre to demonstrate the opportunities that the Pathfinder could build upon in tackling its weak housing market. This was accompanied by an analysis of environmental quality, assessed by way of a commentary on the green space and the presence of neglected and abandoned buildings within the Pathfinder area.

Renew North Staffordshire emphasised the impact on the local housing market of being 'caught' between the three travel-to-work areas of Greater Manchester, Merseyside and the West Midlands, which was exposing it to wide competition for employment and housing. Renew also highlighted the highly fragmented governance structure that is the historical legacy of industrial development in the six separate towns that make up Stoke on Trent. This had led to a more mixed pattern of land use and the proximity of housing to industrial land and transport arteries. Renew recognised that, '...*not all industrial/commercial uses are "good neighbours*"' (RNS, 2004, p. 39).

Another important spatial relationship was highlighted in the competition between neighbourhoods in local housing markets, particularly where it was felt that nearby new supply had undermined the market in more established neighbourhoods. The first round of HMR prospectuses explored in some detail the broader regional implications of these spatial connections, the views of residents on the local housing market, and the factors affecting their decisions to move in or out of the area. Table 4.3 lists some of the main spatial relationships that were routinely identified in the Pathfinders' work.

Table 4.3: Important spatial relationships for Pathfinders

Economic opportunities
- Access to economic opportunities and growth economic sectors.
- Commuting distance and quality and frequency of transport connections.
- Links between local economy and wider regional or national economy.
- Area attractive to long distance, employment-seeking migrants.

Leisure and environmental assets
- Access to countryside or other 'natural' environments.
- Proximity to retail centres offering quality and choice.

Housing market
- Competition with nearby new housing supply.
- Attractiveness of neighbourhood.
- Local demographic and socio-economic characteristics.
- Performance of local housing market (relative to nearby areas).
- Quality of local facilities (e.g., schools) driving local housing market.

Governance and democratic accountability
- Cross-boundary co-operation.
- Joint planning agreements.
- Political 'factionalism' between areas.

Residents' aspirations and intentions

In dealing with the complex nature of the spatial relationships they had identified in their areas, Pathfinders tended to combine both quantitative survey and secondary data sources (such as council tax data) with more qualitative findings. This was particularly the case in Pathfinder work on assessing residents' aspirations and intentions. Bridging NewcastleGateshead used a 2002 housing needs study to identify demand for different types of housing from households wanting to move and from concealed households. It was contended that the housing market in Newcastle and Gateshead was being affected by a polarised age structure. In particular, the intensification of student housing in certain neighbourhoods was identified as contributing to the changed demand for the area, resulting in neighbourhoods being associated with transient demand groups and not being suitable for households with families. The NewcastleGateshead survey demonstrated a low demand for flats. This suggested a need to diversify the stock profile to tackle an ongoing long-term trend for households with children to move out of the Pathfinder area into to the adjacent sub-region. Although its prospectus steered away from providing a benchmark, Partners in Action (Oldham and Rochdale) was one of the few Pathfinders to define housing market vulnerability on the basis of resident responses to a bespoke survey:

> *Housing market vulnerability is defined as the percentage of current residents who wish or plan to leave the neighbourhood in the next 5 years. Within the Pathfinder only 29% expect to and wish to remain in the neighbourhood compared to those outside the Pathfinder area where 46% expect and wish to remain in their neighbourhood. In some of the most vulnerable neighbourhoods this figure rises to around 80% of the respondents planning to or wishing to leave in the next 5 years* (PiA, 2003, p.13).

Like many other Pathfinders, Renew North Staffordshire invested heavily in research underpinning the programme outlined in its prospectus. A *Market Towns New Buyers Survey* provided a representative sample of households in newly-built owner-occupied housing within a 15 mile radius of the conurbation. This survey was used to explore whether adjacent housing development served to displace demand from the HMR area. It found that in general householders had negative perceptions of the urban core. It also demonstrated that a relatively low proportion of households living in new-build housing had previously lived elsewhere in the conurbation. At the same time Renew commissioned a survey of the occupants of new-build properties within the Stoke and Newcastle under Lyme conurbation. This demonstrated very different results from the Market Towns survey, with high levels of demand originating from households already living in the conurbation. In terms of lessons for housing research, these studies demonstrate the importance of having a framework that recognises the dynamics between different parts of the sub-regional housing market and the different aspirations of residents within existing and new and emerging markets. Similar methods, comparing patterns of mobility and household perceptions within and beyond the metropolitan core, were also used by the other Pathfinders. Transform South Yorkshire, commissioned 'insiders' (MRUK, 2004), and 'outsiders' (SQW, 2005), surveys to establish perceptions and demand within the South Yorkshire housing market. The results from these surveys indicated that outsiders tended to have a negative view of the housing offer within the Pathfinder area.

In a pre-HMR survey of leavers, a household survey in Merseyside found that households that had previously lived in Liverpool and had migrated to the Wirral, would not be attracted back to the area even where there were significant investments in the neighbourhoods they had previously lived in (see Lee and Nevin, 2002). In the Bridging NewcastleGateshead Pathfinder, 'housing choice' was cited as a major reason for households migrating to the surrounding sub-region and employment for leaving the region; and in Sandwell and Birmingham (Urban Living), focus groups were used to explore the perceptions of residents living outside the Pathfinder.

Generally, the findings of these various studies implied that whilst efforts should be made to attract people to the area, more emphasis should be placed on retaining households and population and developing a 'housing pathway' (in the loose sense, albeit derived from Clapham's (2002) more formal social constructivist framework), to allow existing residents to remain especially as their economic circumstances and ability to exercise choice improve. This highlighted a tension between the need to respond to existing older and established communities, and the strategy of appealing to the new economy by 're-branding' and 're-packaging' the neighbourhood, to enable the re-calibration of housing and labour markets along the lines discussed earlier in this chapter. Whilst proximity to amenities and quality of life play an important role in determining the trajectory of housing markets and neighbourhoods, the symbolic capital bound up in areas and the perceptions of outsiders are also key drivers. The evidence base assembled by the HMR Pathfinders appears to suggest that whilst changing the areas' profiles may have a long-term impact on changing the trajectory of the area and attracting different household types to it, in the shorter term, the emphasis should be on working with the existing community to develop housing pathways and a long-term vision for the area.

Crime

Crime features as a major driver of housing market performance and was treated in some depth by the Pathfinders in their prospectus submissions. Bridging NewcastleGateshead, for example, identified crime as a significant factor affecting the housing market in its area (BNG, 2003). Levels of crime were differentiated by neighbourhood, demonstrating an unevenness in the types and spatial incidence of crime. Interestingly, their research found that rates of violent crime were low in many neighbourhoods compared to the average for England, and indeed, some neighbourhoods had lower rates than the Newcastle and Gateshead district average. This reinforced the notion that it is the perception and fear of crime, rather than actual incidence, that is often most influential in determining how different areas are viewed. Other Pathfinders used local level data on crime in similar ways. Transform South Yorkshire used crime statistics at small area level to create an index of social cohesion combining population and turnover statistics with crime levels. Meanwhile, Partners in Action drew on existing survey data to suggest that the proportion of residents that thought the borough was a safe place to live had increased over the period 2001-02. The implications of many of the analyses of crime undertaken in the Pathfinders' prospectuses are that housing renewal strategies need to work hard to counteract negative stigmas associated with areas, which may persist long after the 'actual' problem is tackled. In Wood and Vamplew's (1999) study of Teesside, the importance of stigma and negative perceptions are keenly felt, both by residents who often feel that they are unwarranted.

Overcrowding

It must be recalled that the Housing Market Renewal 'agenda' influenced the development of Pathfinder prospectuses, and emphasised the degree of abandonment and 'churning' in the market, as evidence of changing demand and the need for intervention. The emphasis on abandonment, churn and the asymmetry of housing and labour markets (as reflected in house prices) also reflected the politics of HMR and the need to present the most convincing messages to ministers. It is no surprise, therefore, that little attention was paid to the problems of overcrowding in Pathfinder areas. Only two Pathfinders made reference to overcrowding in their submissions and these were generally in areas in which there was a high BME population. Whilst it is not surprising that there was little emphasis on overcrowding, it perhaps explains the emphasis on 'low demand' and 'abandonment' in the Communities Plan, whereas overcrowding depicted a different, but associated problem of changing demand. Overcrowding continues to represent a significant housing stress issue for BME communities, but also characterises the asymmetry between patterns of supply and arising need and the segregation and limited choice in some areas with a high concentration of BME population. This was certainly the case in Birmingham-Sandwell Urban Living, where a pre-HMR report on the North-West Birmingham SRB 6 area indicated a high degree of interaction between overcrowded neighbourhoods in Handsworth and migration to newly-built larger properties in the adjacent local authority of Sandwell (Nevin, Goodson *et al.*, 2001).

Segregation and ethnicity

Whilst the issue of overcrowding was treated parsimoniously, there was considerable attention paid to patterns of ethnic segregation and concentration of ethnic minorities. The availability of 1991 census data, which included for the first time a question on ethnicity, was supplemented by the availability of 2001 data during the production of the prospectuses, and this allowed some limited (although flawed) longitudinal analysis of change in the ethnic composition of neighbourhoods and the broader housing market. Comparison of 'ethnic minority' neighbourhoods was made with other variables such as house prices and empty properties; in PiA, for example, this prompted a number of policy issues regarding the changing demand debate, low demand and segregation:

- Preferences for owner-occupation results in pressure on house prices in existing/traditional areas of residence.
- Household growth amongst BME communities adds to this pressure.
- Movement out of these areas is restricted by social and community ties and fear of harassment, particularly when considering moving into social rented neighbourhoods.
- Danger of social unrest resulting from feelings of social injustice and increased levels of overcrowding, especially in the context of adjacent areas with high levels of empty properties.

A majority of the Pathfinders had relatively low proportions of ethnic minority households compared to the national or regional average. In Liverpool, a number of explanations have been put forward for the problems of low demand, and whilst the relatively low proportion of ethnic minority households (8 per cent), was not the cause of low demand, the absence of a large ethnic minority population was one significant factor in a set of processes that failed to avert the large-scale population decline over the post-war period. In contrast, almost 65 per cent of the Birmingham-Sandwell Pathfinder population was from a Black or Minority Ethnic background, and whilst there were pockets of abandonment and low demand in Birmingham-Sandwell, the problem was more of rapidly changing demand arising from the housing needs of a growing and mobile BME population, in addition to the needs of a large base of asylum seekers and refugees that had been subject to national dispersal policies. This contrasted with the contiguous and high volume of abandonment in areas such as Kensington in Liverpool that had witnessed population loss and accompanied by a relatively low proportion of BME households.

The presence of ethnic minority populations therefore presented significant implications for future household growth and demand within Pathfinders. Partners in Action used a methodology pioneered by Bradford City Council and Ludi Simpson of Manchester University for estimating future growth in the number of households based on the ethnic minority population. PiA also used ODPM's population and household projections to base their analysis of future trajectories and housing needs. The majority of the Pathfinders used existing population trends and projections, and whilst there was some evidence of innovation, the prospectuses signalled the need for more robust and ongoing development of evidence-based data, which is less dependent on inter-census returns in order to track and monitor population change on a consistent and timely basis.

Bringing it together

A number of prospectuses brought the overall analysis together using a range of summary devices such as SWOT analysis (strengths, weaknesses, opportunities and threats) and various forms of indices and domains of housing market weakness. Renew North Staffordshire, for example, utilised a neighbourhood typology to identify the areas of greatest housing weakness across its area development frameworks (ADFs). The indicators used to create the typology included:

- Households with the lowest incomes.
- The lowest house prices and the highest levels of property sales (churning).
- The highest rates of crime and disorder.
- Disproportionate numbers of private renters, students and asylum seekers.
- The highest levels of statutorily unfit properties.
- A proliferation of non-conforming mixed uses.

Transform South Yorkshire grouped domains of indicators together to provide an analysis of *social exclusion*, *social cohesion*, *housing market weakness* and *environmental* indicators. These were mapped at small area level to provide a focal point for investment and areas for intervention. The Manchester-Salford prospectus provided a commentary on the features of low and changing demand and how this has shaped the housing and neighbourhood offer within the Pathfinder. It was based on a comprehensive set of indicators and is a good example of the way in which housing market analysis can be brought together in a summary fashion to demonstrate the collective understanding of the situation locally. The Manchester-Salford Pathfinder used these to maximum effect by concentrating on the narrative and how these indicators related them to the need for interventions, action plans and areas for investment. Alongside this was a summary of the evidence for each ADF and how the planned interventions would make a difference in each area was provided. SWOT analysis was embedded in a variety of different narratives of housing markets and their performance within each of the prospectuses; PiA and Manchester-Salford were more explicit in summarising the strengths, weakness, opportunities and threats within their respective markets (see Table 4.4).

Weighing up the influence of these local factors against other, more consistent, sets of drivers is difficult, however, and examples of locally specific factors included: the role of deep mining and the 30 metre rule affecting house prices within North Staffordshire (Renew), and the historical legacy and path dependency of 'Tyneside flats' in Bridging NewcastleGateshead's submission. Urban Living provided a summary of key market drivers with symptoms and a baseline position for each indicator (see Table 4.5).

Table 4.4: Comparative SWOT analysis of MSP and PiA prospectuses

Strengths	PiA	MSP	Opportunities	PiA	MSP	Weaknesses	PiA	MSP	Threats	PiA	MSP
Proximity to town or regional centre/countryside	X	X	Strong growth in the regional centre (knowledge economy)	X	X	High economic inactivity and benefit dependency/low income	X	X	Continued out-migration by families		X
Assets of regional centre		X	Completion of planned investments in schools, transport and/or health	X	X	Declining population and families leaving		X	Displacement by investment outside HMRP	X	X
Committed investment in public services		X							Transport improvements lead to commuting into regional centre		X
High levels of private sector investment in commercial and housing developments across the city	X	X	High prices in other areas so HMRP represents value for money family housing	X	X	Poor quality physical environment, aspect/maintenance	X	X	Unregulated private sector undermines HMRP and other investment		X
LAs with track record of delivering change		X	Interest from developers in large-scale investment		X	Poor quality social infrastructure, especially schools	X	X	Macro-economic conditions change	X	X
Coherent funding strategies across the LAs		X	Key workers – retaining economically active working in the city		X	Lack of housing choice, age and obsolescence	X	X	Image and perception of the boroughs and neighbourhoods	X	
Good transport links	X		Household growth	X		Opportunities for the private sector piecemeal and small scale	X		Low skills base unable to take up job opportunities	X	
Population remains and voids low	X		An improving schools performance	X		Below average educational performance	X		Unnecessary or premature release of greenfield sites for residential development	X	
Communities with strong cultural and social bonds	X		Joint Vision and borough Masterplanning	X		Perception of crime and image of neighbourhoods	X		Potential lack of suitable building land in the HMR area in the longer term	X	
Communities with a sense of place and pride	X		Improving transport	X		High turnover in social rented housing	X				
Population young and diverse	X					Polarisation and segregation of communities	X				

PiA: Partners in Action; MSP: Manchester-Salford Partnership.
Note: PiA identifies sources to support its SWOT analysis.
Source: authors' comparison of prospectuses.

Table 4.5: Summary of housing market drivers in Birmingham-Sandwell

Key market drivers	Typical symptoms	Examples of baseline position
People: demographic and economic change	Loss of population	6% decline in population 1991-2001
	Increase in BME communities	Over 90,000 new BME residents (39% growth 1991-2001)
	Decline in manufacturing jobs	Decline in manufacturing jobs (Sandwell 49% in 1981 → 26% in 2001)
	Low wages/incomes	Mean household income 16% below Birmingham/Sandwell
	Loss of skilled workers	40% of population has no qualifications
	Increase in dependent population	23% of all households, include someone disabled or long-term sick
	Loss of 'family' age groups	Decline 1991-2001 0.3% HMRA (13.4% decline WB/GG)
	Levels of asylum seekers/refugees	8 x concentration of NASS contracts in Pathfinder area compared with Birmingham/Sandwell as a whole
	Growth of private rented sector	Private rented sector 10% HMRA 7% Birmingham/Sandwell (2001)
Perceptions: rising aspirations in the housing market	Increase in home ownership	GB 49.1% to 68.1% (1971-2001) HMRA 49% (2001)
	Preference for large properties	35% moving want a larger house
	Negative perceptions of inner city neighbourhoods	68% of existing households likely to move or show preference to leave area
	Negative external perceptions of HMRA	External perceptions are that the area is run down, with poor housing quality and choice, poor facilities and services, and high levels of crime
	Higher levels of affordability	Total household income (£/capita) increased by 17.38% from 1995-1999
Property: inability to restructure housing provision	Lack of new housing supply	670 completions in HMRA area in last 3 years
	Dominance of social renting	37% LA + RSL in HMRA area (28% Birmingham/Sandwell)
	High desire to leave area	68% of existing households preference is to move out of area
	Predominance of lower-value properties	75% of transaction below £50,000, 5% above £100,000 UK average house price £150,000 (Average price 61% of WM regional figure)
	Level of unfit housing	15% in Sandwell – 7.6% nationally
Place: inadequate public services/dysfunctional urban form	Relatively poor education offer	Only 35.2% of pupils 5 or more GCSE's A*-C passes
	Dissatisfaction with neighbourhoods	17% of households dissatisfied with neighbourhood
	Unkempt and untidy local environment	18% of households dissatisfied with area around property
	Relatively poor health levels	Infant mortality 20% above national average. Life expectancy 2.5 years less than national average
	High crime levels/anti-social behaviour	Incidents of arson 1.84/1,000 properties (1.04/1,000 for rest of Birmingham/Sandwell)

Source: Urban Living Prospectus, 2003, p.41.

Whilst there are no examples of specific models of neighbourhood trajectories to anticipate what the market for particular neighbourhoods will be in the future, there are some examples of Pathfinders providing commentaries on the anticipated future profile of parts of the Pathfinder. For example, Renew provided a profile of key demographic statistics (including household type, ethnicity, and employment status) against its 'social housing' neighbourhood typologies (such as 'social periphery' and 'social core') and speculated that, '...*in time the estates will become more unstable as demography creates vacancies*' (RNS, 2004, p.55). In Renew's case this was supported by evidence on incomes and average mortgage payments and rental payments within different parts of the Pathfinder which provided a commentary on the competition between tenures to provide further background on the trajectory of neighbourhoods:

> *The continuing market for the terraced sector in Stoke-on-Trent is dependent upon the sub-regions low wage economy. The Inland Revenue data base records the average income as the third lowest of the 354 local authorities on their records. Evidence from the household surveys highlights average mortgage repayments of between £36 to £55 per week in areas in the first phase of the Market Renewal Programme. By way of comparison, in Meir [a suburb of Stoke] council house rents are £49 and private rented accommodation £63 per week. Therefore, the cheapest accommodation for a low wage employee in Stoke-on-Trent is the pre 1919 terraced property* (RNS, 2004, p.56).

Developing in-house expertise and the 'collective memory of place'

All of the prospectuses were founded upon some element of newly commissioned work. Renew North Staffordshire, for example, commissioned a number of bespoke reports including 'The Economic Futures for North Staffordshire and their implications for the Market Renewal Area', which informed the development of the prospectus and were published as separate appendices to their prospectus. However, there was also considerable use of existing data sources and systems, whose principle purpose was not housing market analysis, but which was brought to bear on the housing market question. Some Pathfinders such as the Manchester-Salford Partnership were able to begin to explore the use of council tax data as a means of measuring turnover (in addition to vacancy rates), although this has not become a widespread practice, due to inconsistencies in the way that council tax datasets are maintained. However, as we noted in the previous chapter, the environment in which data from sources such local council tax registers can be used has changed, with a risk averse environment predominating and public service agreements creating obstacles to shared intelligence and data. This is a topic we return to in the conclusions where we discuss the development of data management systems and foresight.

The development of HMR prospectuses led to a number of cross-boundary initiatives designed to understand the local housing market and to share intelligence.

In Liverpool (NewHeartlands), the designation of HMR status subsequently led to the development of an asset management database on facilities and land-use, which was used extensively in the development of the prospectus and implementation of HMR. In South Yorkshire, TSY (Transform South Yorkshire) merged its research and intelligence function with the existing sub-regional housing and regeneration partnership SYHARP, developing an evidence base for the sub-region based on best practice of the monitoring of the housing market locally. These arenas will become more important in the future not just as reception areas for data but also as mechanisms through which data and interpretation of data can be challenged. The infrastructure and data sharing mechanisms of HMR (across boundaries and across themes) is a lasting legacy which was demonstrated within the first wave of HMR prospectuses. This has had the effect of creating a more systematic focal point for the Pathfinder for understanding the local dynamics of declining markets, but also provides a basis for capturing the collective memory of place: the trajectories and changing fortunes of places, and how they are shaped by events.

Summary

This chapter has focused on the development of the initial wave of prospectuses which reflected a large volume of activity in the research and intelligence gathering of housing market processes and outcomes locally. More significantly, data was harmonised systematically across local authority boundaries and the findings placed within a broader spatial framework of the sub-region and region. The language of Housing Market Renewal and the prospectuses consistently favoured radical interventions in order to provide 'housing pathways', to 'reconnect communities to the emerging economy', and to close the gap in housing prices between parts of the sub-region and HMR area. This provided a fertile collective mood favouring demolition as a major tool for restructuring the housing market.

CHAPTER 5:
Taking stock: Housing Market Renewal interventions and early impact

Introduction

In the previous chapter, we argued that HMR prospectuses proceeded to build up a core narrative that demonstrated and evaluated the extent of 'asymmetry' between the housing and labour markets, and the type and extent of intervention needed to re-calibrate these two 'systems'. As we have already seen, the HMR fund was the result of an intense period of research and lobbying for the need to address structural, geographically widespread and multi-faceted problems in the housing market (Lee and Nevin, 2003; HC 240-I, 2001-02). In recognition of the complexity of the issues and the long time-frame between intervention and outcomes, HMR was intended to be, and remains, a long-term policy with programmes running typically until 2018. In reflecting on the impact of HMR, our perspective is relatively constrained as we are only about halfway through the programme's planned intervention period, with much work to be done over the next decade. Within this context we consider three issues in this chapter:

1. **Interventions and the delivery of HMR Pathfinders to date:** the Pathfinders made a case for significant amounts of clearance and demolition to deal with low demand – how much of the original plans have been delivered and what impact has this had to date?
2. **The HMR project going forward:** how has the housing market and policy environment affected the low-demand debate, altered the thrust of policy, and exposed weaknesses in the HMR 'project'? Although envisaged as a 15 year programme, some of the areas within Pathfinder boundaries may no longer require intervention of the kind originally planned. It is relevant at this point to return to the original rationale for the programme, to look at the changes in markets since then, and to consider the criticisms of HMR clearance programmes, which in some cases led to a *volte face* by Pathfinders.
3. **Problems attendant to any evaluations of programmes such as HMR:** particularly where their outcomes and objectives are long term in their nature, and where the policy foci and priorities – like the market itself – are constantly in flux.

Pathfinder activities and delivery

In seeking to reshape local housing markets, demolition was seen as highly necessary right from the start of the low-demand debate, and certainly in the construction of the evidence base for HMR and the dissemination period running up to the launch of the programme. Whilst the 'risk' analysis (see Chapter 3) contained in the M62 Corridor Study (and subsequent regional housing market analyses), did not purport to be a route map for the bulldozer, demolition was discussed enthusiastically during this period as a primary tool and a means of addressing what was perceived and touted to be the 'last chance' to get regeneration and renewal right in the areas identified as having housing market weakness.

Demolition was identified by all Pathfinders as part of the strategic 'toolkit' of HMR interventions. It was, however, but one of several options and Pathfinders had at their disposal a reasonably wide range of other ways that they could spend their funds and address market failure. The original intention behind the policy was that there would be a sufficient range of intervention options available to Pathfinders in order that they might respond flexibly to differing local market conditions, contexts and 'drivers of change'. The local strategic frameworks by which interventions were to be structured were, arguably, considered to be more important than the imposition of a strict template of interventions. ODPM's assessment of the Pathfinders' initial prospectuses and its subsequent negotiations with Pathfinders on funding focused on local HMR strategies, the evidence underpinning them and strategic aspects of delivery including phasing, value for money, risk assessment and governance.

Although it was recognised that housing market weakness was not solely a product of deficiencies in the quality or demand for *housing*, HMR funds could not be used to directly fund *non-housing* improvements. But their availability for demolition, new build, site acquisition, master planning and related environmental works nevertheless constituted significant flexibility compared to traditional housing programmes. Furthermore, the ability of Pathfinders to recycle their capital receipts[4] added a degree of financial independence to this flexibility. The capital nature of the programme and the ineligibility of funds for the support of revenue streams should be stressed as an original feature of the HMR programme that has endured. The Audit Commission (2005) identified three broad types of HMR interventions being undertaken:

- **Stock clearance and site assembly:** including acquisition (e.g., through compulsory purchase powers), demolition and land assembly with the provision of compensation packages to enable these interventions.
- **Physical improvements:** including private sector housing renewal, renovation, environmental improvements and measures to 'design out' crime.
- **Improvements to social cohesion and human capital:** including neighbourhood management, landlord accreditation, construction skills and training.

4   The re-use of monies earned from the disposal of assets such as land or acquired housing stock. Normally such receipts are claimed by the national Exchequer.

Interventions aimed at large-scale change, such as through the acquisition and demolition of properties, are possibly what really marks HMR out as different to previous approaches, as well as its cross-tenure approach which meant that the programme affected tightly bound communities and coterminous housing arrangements irrespective of the nature of ownership.

It is interesting to note that, whilst demolition was the aspect of HMR that really marked it out from other contemporary housing and regeneration interventions and was a universal element of strategy, only four of the Pathfinders set out specific targets for demolition and clearance in their initial prospectuses. Together, these four Pathfinders – Renew North Staffordshire, NewHeartlands, Elevate East Lancashire and Partners in Action – were proposing almost 40,000 demolitions (Table 5.1). The variation in local delivery (as opposed to a nationally prescribed programme) is reflected in Table 5.1: for example, NewHeartlands emphasised new build and demolition but no refurbishment programme – perhaps an indication of a wholesale 'modernisation' programme; whereas Renew North Staffordshire planned for a very large refurbishment programme. Partners in Action, meanwhile, planned for a net gain in housing stock following its demolition programme, which was designed to address 'changing demand' in its market, whereas the other Pathfinders were planning for a net loss to tackle 'low demand'.

Table 5.1: Summary of lifetime programme outputs in initial prospectuses of selected Pathfinders

	Renew North Staffordshire	Elevate East Lancashire	Partners in Action	NewHeartlands	Total
Demolitions:					
Private	11,877		978	12,126	24,981
Social	2,550		1,494	8,529	12,573
Other	74				74
Total	**14,501**	**1,569**	**2,472**	**20,655**	**39,197**
New build:					
Private	7,480		2,680	14,271	24,431
LCHO	3,354			4,254	7,608
Social	1,694		725		2,419
Total	**12,528**	**314**	**3,405**	**18,525**	**34,772**
Refurbishments:					
Social	25,757		3,154		28,911
Private	9,710		1,778		11,488
Total	**35,467**	**2,719**	**4,932**		**43,118**

Source: Pathfinder prospectuses published between October 2003 and October 2004.

In total, the Pathfinders claimed and spent around £1.2 billion of HMR grant between 2003 and 2008. Table 5.2 to Table 5.5 provide a summary of the programme's principal capital outputs since 2003. The main output in terms of the volume of housing units affected by the programme has been refurbishments to properties, in many cases contributing to meeting the Decent Homes Standard. By April 2008, around 50,000 properties had been subject to some form of refurbishment work, generally aimed at modernising dwellings so that they better met residents' needs, and also so that they were less 'obsolete' in the local housing market (Table 5.4). In this sense, refurbishments met the twin aims of improving existing conditions in neighbourhoods as well as renewing the local housing market.

However, the focus of HMR was leading towards a modernisation and competitiveness agenda, which meant that the option of refurbishment appeared to dilute the potential to 'recreate' housing markets, provide a clean break with the past and promote re-branding and image for Pathfinder housing markets and neighbourhoods. Demolition provided an opportunity to recast and re-brand neighbourhoods in order to insert Pathfinder areas into the merging economic narrative (e.g., the knowledge and creative economy), and to improve their 'competitiveness'.

The acquisition and demolition of properties, whilst being the most controversial element of the programme, was at the same time one of its most important features. Up to 2008, HMR funds were used to demolish fewer than 13,000 dwellings, mostly in order to clear sites in preparation for replacement housing, normally of a different type, size or tenure than had previously been located on the cleared site. This represents a substantial output although is far short of the scale of demolition that was originally envisaged by commentators at the outset of the programme: of the 40,000 demolitions proposed in the prospectuses of Elevate, NewHeartlands, Partners in Action and Renew, fewer than nine per cent (3,494) had been achieved by the end of 2007/08 financial year (see Table 5.5). Given that most demolition was to take place in the early years of the programme to facilitate site assembly and remediation, it is reasonable to suggest that the final figure on clearance is close to being reached, and that it represents a significant scaling back of the programme in the face of criticisms and a changing national policy context (see below). It is certainly far short of the type of radical restructuring that was suggested by some interpretations of the original 'changing demand' evidence base. Nevertheless, given that these demolitions have occurred over a five year period, and only in certain intervention areas, their impact on local market structures is likely to be significant.

Over the same period, it can be seen that fewer than 1,900 new homes were provided on cleared sites (Table 5.4). This has clearly not equalled the level of demolitions, although there is a sequencing logic that explains this. Indeed, it can be seen from a comparison of Table 5.2 and Table 5.3 that the performance of Pathfinders was generally improving by 2007/08, and they were increasing the number of new housing completions. This performance preceded the economic downturn, of course, which went on to have such a devastating impact on housing development activity and severely challenged Pathfinders' strategies. Table 5.5 gives a slightly different impression of the performance of the Pathfinders. Whereas Table 5.2 to Table 5.4 are assembled from Audit Commission Performance Reviews, Table 5.5 is constructed from the annual reports by the Pathfinders themselves. Included in some of the reporting is the delivery of refurbishments and new homes on HMR land, but not financed by HMR.

Differences in the reported outputs make the task of evaluating their impacts more complex. It is clear that the Pathfinders acquired a significant amount of land (114 acres) and roughly 12,000 dwellings; the fact that Pathfinders delivered land remediation and levered private sector investment is an important aspect of the Pathfinder intervention, and is consistent with the initial objectives of the programme. However, this important part of the process of HMR appears to be missing from the official (Audit Commission) accounts: the delivery of new homes facilitated by HMR, but funded privately, is illustrative of the regeneration and renewal opportunities and potential that the programme brought to bear. It is helpful to recall that CLG's Land Use Change Statistics (LUCS) analysed in the baseline evaluation report on HMR demonstrated how Pathfinder areas had been subject to little investment or change in land use patterns over a 25 to 30 year period indicated by additions or demolitions to the housing stock (Leather *et al.*, 2007). The acquisition of land and the leverage of private sector investment was a major aim of the Pathfinders in order to close the gap between the local housing and labour markets, and to address the weakness of the market in these areas.

However, there are major issues of accountability and strategic alignment raised by the development of non-HMR funded activity within the Pathfinders' boundaries. Was this housing aligned with the objectives of the Pathfinders and who was it marketed towards? Many of the Pathfinders are adjacent to, or intersect, their respective city centres and the delivery of housing on these sites may appear to fit with 'expressed demand' of the market (e.g., buy to let), and the vision for delivering housing that meets the needs of the knowledge-based and 'creative' economy. The Manchester-Salford Partnership is a good example of this alignment. Table 5.5 indicates that almost 11,000 new homes were built, although the amount delivered through HMR funds was significantly below this figure, with fewer than 500 in 2007/08. Therefore, whilst HMR had a potentially positive impact in levering private sector investment and delivering new build, the flip side of this is the alignment and displacement effects with wider HMR objectives. These issues of displacement and 'effective demand' are picked up again in the conclusions.

Table 5.2: Summary of Pathfinder outputs, 2007/08

2007/08	HMR funding claimed (£ m)	Refurbishments	Acquisitions	Demolitions	New homes	Performance
Bridging NewcastleGateshead	40.9	1,623	175	289	124	Performing well
Elevate East Lancashire	48.8	506	384	272	0	Performing adequately
Gateway Hull & East Riding	24.9	410	165	62	69	Performing well
Manchester-Salford Partnership	53.8	Unknown	540	Unknown	473	Performing strongly
NewHeartlands Merseyside	50.8	599	422	256	301	Performing strongly
Partners in Action Oldham Rochdale	37.4	454	174	148	165	Performing well
Renew North Staffordshire	38.4	2,544	466	282	52	Performing strongly
Transform South Yorkshire	48.7	Unknown	Unknown	Unknown	Unknown	Unknown
Urban Living Birmingham Solihull	29.2	2,262	132	207	36	Performing well
TOTAL	**372.9**	**8,398**	**2,458**	**1,516**	**1,220**	

Note: HMR funding only, 2006-2008.
Source: Audit Commission Performance Reports.

Table 5.3: Summary of Pathfinder outputs, 2006/07

2006/07	HMR funding claimed (£ m)	Refurbishments	Acquisitions	Demolitions	New homes	Performance
Bridging NewcastleGateshead	23.0	1,692	115	258	44	Performing well
Elevate East Lancashire	46.0	390	633	323	39	Performing adequately
Gateway Hull & East Riding	16.3	20	146	92	44	Performing adequately
Manchester-Salford Partnership	52.1	2,309	601	755	Unknown	Performing strongly
NewHeartlands Merseyside	47.0	2,300	650	772	Unknown	Performing strongly
Partners in Action Oldham Rochdale	30.0	296	211	161	106	Performing adequately
Renew North Staffordshire	29.0	846	300	215		Performing well
Transform South Yorkshire	41.2	1,751	384	525	176	Performing well
Urban Living Birmingham Solihull	15.2	518	70	60	52	Performing adequately
TOTAL	**299.8**	**10,122**	**3,110**	**3,161**	**461**	

Note: HMR funding only, 2006-2008.
Source: Audit Commission Performance Reports.

Table 5.4: Summary of programme outputs, 2003-2008

	HMR funding claimed	Refurbishments	Acquisitions	Demolitions	New homes	Source
2003-2006	£552m	30,644	Unknown	8,053	159	Pathfinder chairs (2006)
2006/07	£300m	10,122	3,110	3,161	461	Table 5.2
2007/08	£373m	8,398	2,458	1,516	1,220	Table 5.3
TOTAL 2003-2008	**£1,225m**	**49,164**	**Unknown**	**12,730**	**1,840**	

Table 5.5: Pathfinder delivery and performance, 2003/04-2007/08 (from published accounts)

	BNG	EEL	Gateway	MSP	NH	PiA	TSY	RENEW	UL	Total
a) Properties demolished:	1,850	1,296	331	2,837	911	494	1,732	793	644	10,888
*Private**	*45%*		*46%*		*65%*	*24%*	*8%*		*103*	*30%*
*Social**	*55%*		*54%*		*35%*	*76%*	*92%*		*541*	*70%*
b) Properties improved/ refurbished (all)	4,013	2,346	352	10,840	9,187	2,536	1,915	5,393	8,905	45,487
c) New homes built	170	1,257	144	10,950	17	298	2	52	197	13,087
d) Dwellings acquired:	627	1,883	442	2,996	2,417	759	0	1,129	1,608	11,861
Private	*98*			*0*	*1,616*	*133*	*0*		*413*	*(2,260)*
e) Land acquired (hectares)	10.53	8	8	47	13	10	0	1	15	114
f) Total spend (£m)	123.8	160.8	49.9	187.7	183.7	115.6	43.9	86.7	88.8	1,041
g) Cost per property built/ improved (f/c+b)	£29,603	£44,632	£100,605	£8,613	£19,954	£40,779	£22,922	£15,925	£9,762	£17,772

Note: figures are for 2004/05 to 2007/08 except Bridging NewcastleGateshead and Manchester-Salford Partnership where annual reports for 2003/04 are included.
* Percentage share of demolitions, where known.
Source: annual HMR reports available from Pathfinders.

Growing criticism of the Pathfinder programme

The demolition of housing (particularly social housing) and the delivery of new private housing raised concerns about the displacement of households in housing need and whether this constituted a form of state sponsored gentrification. The problem was considered to be particularly acute given that house prices began to rise rapidly in Pathfinder areas. Table 5.5 indicates (where data are available) that a significant proportion of demolitions and acquisitions was social housing (over 90 per cent in Transform South Yorkshire's case). Some commentators were therefore quick to point out the apparent paradox between promoting sustainable communities, while backing a programme of market renewal that was using demolition as one of its main tools. This was a paradox that was not lost on residents or the national press.[5] The early days of the HMR programme were faltering in comparison to the more tangible signs of delivery of new homes that were seen in the couple of years up to 2007/08. To an extent this is understandable, not least because of local sensitivities and the need for careful community involvement. The scale and nature of Pathfinders' plans inevitably necessitated a period of 'gearing up' through consultation, masterplanning, policy alignment, land and housing acquisition – including compulsory purchase processes – and other preparatory activities. Physical works, such as demolition and the provision of replacement housing, naturally, were only possible once these preparatory works were under way.

However, questions began to arise as to the efficacy of demolition and the necessity of such intervention. In parliament, Lord Alton of Liverpool asked of the extent of opposition to HMR that was growing during the summer of 2005:

> How many residents and tenants' groups and non-governmental organisations have expressed opposition to the Pathfinder programme; what are those groups and organisations; and on what grounds the Ancient Monuments Society, English Heritage, the Victorian Society, the Council for British Archaeology, the Heritage Trust for the Northwest, Save Britain's Heritage and the Prince's Trust opposed Pathfinder projects[?] (Hansard: HL Deb, 22 June 2005, c174W).

The level of formal criticism received by government appeared to be marginal, with Baroness Andrews for the government responding that the Office of the Deputy Prime Minister had received:

> ...five ministerial letters from residents via their MP and one from a non-governmental body, the Merseyside Civic Trust, opposing the housing market renewal programme. In other correspondence we have received approximately 25 letters and e-mails voicing similar opposition or concerns. One of these letters was

---

5   See *The Sunday Times Magazine*, 19 September 2004, 'The Madness of John Prescott'; *The Daily Telegraph*, 29 January 2005, 'Prescott's Bulldozers Ready to Demolish Victorian Terraces' and other similar national press articles.

from the Spital Hill Local Voice group based in Sheffield...The Ancient Monuments Society, the Victorian Society, the Council for British Archaeology, the Heritage Trust for the Northwest and the Prince's Trust have not expressed a formal view to the Government on the HMR programme. Save Britain's Heritage gave evidence in the recent Office of the Deputy Prime Minister Select Committee on Empty Homes and Low Demand Pathfinders (Hansard, HL Deb, 22 June 2005, c175W).

Lord Alton also challenged the government on whether a systematic process was being followed that complied with Environmental Impact Regulations, when making decisions about demolition and the compulsory purchase of properties. Baroness Andrews, again responding on behalf of the government, said that decisions about which property to compulsorily purchase, demolish, refurbish or leave remain the responsibility of:

...the local authority concerned as the statutory body, informed by the Pathfinder strategy. Plans for different types of intervention, including decisions to proceed with demolition of properties, are not taken on the basis of simple drive-by surveys. They are informed by various factors, including neighbourhood renewal assessment (or other similar comprehensive assessment), community views, analyses of supply and demand, housing stock condition, demographics (Hansard, *op. cit.*).

Such exchanges reflected a growing hostility towards HMR and negative press exposure to the policy. The hostility was fuelled during a period in which the national housing market 'boom' was reaching Pathfinder areas, driving prices up and affordability down. In a September 2005 edition of *Regeneration and Renewal*, it was reported that the NewHeartlands Pathfinder had updated its prospectus submission to ODPM, and scaled back its forecast clearance with plans to demolish 7,000 fewer homes than originally proposed over the scheme's lifetime. This was partly in response to rising average house prices, which in the area covered by the Pathfinder had more than doubled from £30,000 to £61,000 over the three year period to 2005 (Willis, 2005, p.9):

There are a number of factors [behind the lower demolition rates] *one being that we have more sophisticated databases. But also the increases in housing prices mean we can't do as much as we had hoped in acquiring properties* (NewHeartlands spokesman in *op. cit.*, p.9).

Despite the growing disparity between resources and acquisition costs, making it more difficult to implement demolition, a narrative was developing that saw demolition as unnecessary. Stories abounded of perfectly habitable dwellings falling victim to the demolition ball, adding to a popular groundswell against the policy. Attacks were made on the evidence base and those seen as responsible for highlighting market failure and promoting demolition. Save Britain's Heritage, for example, identified a dissonance between the academics and policy-makers producing the evidence base on the one side, and the communities affected by their evidence and recommendations, on the other:

> *The so-called problem of market failure was identified and studied by the Centre for Urban Research [sic] at Birmingham University (CURS). It estimated 1.5 million homes to be at risk of market failure, of which 850,000 are in Pathfinder areas. It has called for up to 400,000 for these to be cleared away. These figures have been accepted by the Office of the Deputy Prime Minister in the policy document "The Northern Way" and its September 2004 follow-up "Moving it Forward: The Northern Way", launched by John Prescott. These documents are the counterbalance to the ODPM's "Sustainable Communities Plan" which sees massive increases in house construction in the South-East. Current rates of clearance will see 167,000 houses demolished over the 15 year period of Pathfinder, yet the Pathfinders are calling for more...these academics are detached from the despair and wrath of the threatened communities* (Save Britain's Heritage, 2006, p.11).

The report called for a stop to demolitions on the basis that the evidence was out of date and no longer relevant:

> *Pathfinder [sic] is a policy based on research that is out of date. Most of the initial research into housing market conditions was carried out before the current boom in the housing market (op. cit., p.57).*

Websites such as Corporate Watch (see Figure 5.1) began to identify house builders and developers as beneficiaries of what it saw as a 'revanchist' state, in other words, one which was sponsoring a process of gentrification as a form of 'global urban strategy' aimed at furthering middle-class interests (after Smith, 1996). Dedicated websites appeared in response to individual Pathfinder proposals (such as Fight for Our Homes, part of the resistance to Elevate East Lancashire's plans), and more established organisations such as the Victorian Society discussed the threat of HMR to the British vernacular housing form, asking rather rhetorically in an article in March 2006 whether the Victorian terrace was an 'endangered species' (Victorian Society, 2006).

The 2007 baseline evaluation report on HMR acknowledged the negative coverage of demolition and clearance activity, but also found that:

> *...overall, local residents have supported plans for neighbourhood remodelling, but a minority of households can demand considerable time and resources from pathfinder and local authority delivery teams. Whilst community engagement and involvement have always been important strategic objectives for the pathfinders, they are facing new challenges* (Leather et al., 2007, p.xxi).

Figure 5.1: Corporate Watch website

Source: Corporate Watch (2009).

While some of the criticisms of HMR policy are justified, the most vocal voices have not necessarily been those of residents. Architects, urban historians, heritage campaigners and even a former rock star[6] have waded into the debate, usually with an emphasis on aspects of 'community' that are very difficult to pin down, yet are understandably emotive. The perceived advantages of traditional communities and of life in decades past is often evoked. Chris Allen's (2008) highly critical study of HMR in Liverpool, for example, is predicated largely on perpetuating a notion of social class (and its importance in the reproduction of society), that New Labour explicitly disavowed. Allen argues, in essence, that the 'working class' views housing in a way that is fundamentally different to the way the 'middle class' does. The realities of this are likely to be far more complex than this simple class analysis suggests. Putting to one side the argument about whether the 'working class' still

---

6   Following negative publicity involving the potential demolition of the musician Ringo Starr's childhood home in Liverpool, ODPM's Permanent Secretary Dame Mavis McDonald promised that a survey of the value of historic properties would be carried out before any more were demolished.

exists in the same form that it once may have, Allen's views on the form and function of housing run counter to much of the evidence of the increasing importance of housing as a locus for investment (and not just community and family), among a broad, and widening, section of the population. Whether this reflects an innate desire for ownership, as an extension of the purported 'ontological security' of home ownership via its investment and remunerative potential (see Saunders, 1990), or whether it reflects the results of policy (the promotion of a property owning democracy), it nevertheless explains the enormous expansion of owner-occupation over the past century, a trend that has only recently abated. Local housing surveys routinely record high levels of aspiration for owner-occupation, and sociologists such as Allen have found the increasing socio-cultural significance of housing (not least in the popular media) to be fertile grounds for discussion.

In this light, market renewal appears an overtly deterministic and linear, or modernist mode of regeneration, inviting comparisons with the comprehensive redevelopment programmes of the 1960s. However, the realities of the relationship between local housing markets, neighbourhoods and economic function appear to be rarely engaged with by the critics of HMR. In the context of disruption to residents' lives these strategic concerns may appear to be obtuse and abstract aims. This highlights the inevitable tension between evidence, strategy and engagement at the heart of the programme. Very negative (national) press coverage at the time of a much reduced Labour majority following the 2005 general election made central government think twice about the future of the policy and it reined in control over some aspects. Interestingly, local media coverage has – on the whole – been more ambivalent, partly in recognition of the dire situation that some neighbourhoods had fallen into and therefore the potential of any form of regeneration to redress this. It would appear that the pragmatic response to these concerns has been to focus on the nature of the *qualitative* mismatch between supply, for example, its quality and the choice available; and demand, including the aspirations as well as needs of different demand groups. It must also be recalled that, in some cases, there was popular support both in local newspapers and amongst the general public for demolition and clearance (see Figure 2.6 in Chapter 2) prior to the implementation of HMR. This may be attributed to a fear of the impact of low demand on house prices amongst the enlarged property owning democracy.

Measuring the impact of HMR in an era of growth and increased supply

Nevertheless, the ongoing relevance of the HMR strategy came under increasing scrutiny as national housing and planning policy turned its attention to delivering a 'step change' in new supply. The changing market conditions, together with the incessant criticism of the programme, forced Pathfinders to reduce their demolition targets as the affordability problem worsened. Documents began to refer to a reduced demolition target, from 400,000 to between 70,000 and 100,000 dwellings over 15 years. It was becoming clear following the Barker Reviews of housing supply and land use planning (Barker, 2004; 2006), that a new period had been entered, marked by an overriding concern with new housing supply to address affordability problems and concerns.

In 1997, each of England's regions had a lower-quartile house price to lower-quartile earnings ratio (the government's preferred measure of affordability) of around 3 to 4:1. By 2006, the England average stood at around 7:1, ranging from 5:1 in the North East to over 8.5:1 in London and the South (NHPAU, 2007). Since 1992, price rises averaged 7.4 per cent per annum in the UK – peaking at 17 per cent in 2002 (Figure 5.2) – a rate considerably higher than in other Western European countries. The Barker Review of Housing Supply (Barker, 2004) concluded that, '...*higher and more responsive levels of house building, leading to a lower trend in real house prices, would benefit the UK in economic terms*' (*op. cit.*, p.11). Irrespective of the impact of the credit crunch in stabilising and effectively reducing prices, affordability problems do still remain. This began to raise important questions about the future of renewal activity and regeneration programmes such as HMR (Ferrari, 2007).

Figure 5.2: House price inflation in the United Kingdom, 1980-2006

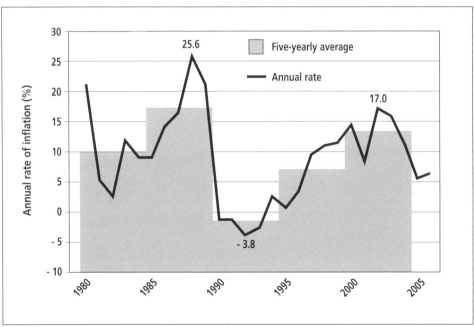

Source: CLG Live Table 502.
Note: data are mix adjusted, but are from different sources as follows: 1980-92: 5% survey of building societies; 1993-2003: 5% survey of mortgage lenders; 2003-04: survey of mortgage lenders; 2005-06: Regulated Mortgage Survey.

Revised planning policy guidance for housing, PPS 3 (CLG, 2006a), was explicitly designed to enable the planning system to become a more proactive agent in the delivery of new housing. Furthermore, it is clear that the government at this time viewed housing policy of significant importance, reflected in the Minister for Housing (The Rt. Hon. Margaret Beckett), being allocated a chair at the cabinet table for the first time in recent history. What is clear is that, whilst initially the HMR programme set out an ambitious demolition programme, affordability issues had pulled housing up the political agenda, and therefore the scale of demolition was subsequently reduced significantly and the programme was set on a course of more sensitive consultation. At the time of writing, most of the HMR Pathfinders were in their seventh programme year. Although many of their interventions cannot be expected to fully impact on the housing market for some years to come, we can nevertheless take stock of the early progress that was made in tackling the problems of empty properties, low house prices, turnover and out-migration. In addressing this question, and the broader one of the impact of the Pathfinders' work today, we briefly draw on work undertaken as part of the National Evaluation of HMR (Leather *et al.*, 2007) together with the Audit Commission's findings from its ongoing programme of scrutiny of the Pathfinders' activities and published accounts from the Pathfinder programme.

Figure 5.3: Vacancy rate, 2001-2006

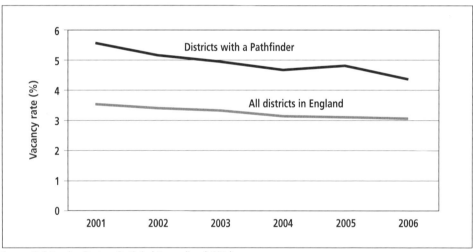

Source: CLG Housing Strategy Statistical Appendices (HSSAs).
Note: 'Districts with a Pathfinder' excludes the East Riding of Yorkshire, because only a very small proportion of that district falls within a Pathfinder.

Vacancy rates in Pathfinder districts fell at a faster rate than in other districts across England between 2001-06 (Figure 5.3). Most local authorities with a Pathfinder reported that the incidence of low demand in their area had been decreasing (Figure 5.4). This measure, which includes an assessment of various demand indicators, suggests that turnover has been stabilising, the incidence of refused offers for social housing has been decreasing, and waiting lists have lengthened.

Figure 5.4: Local authority estimates of social rented properties in low demand

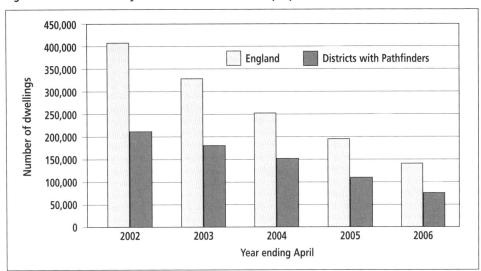

Source: CLG Housing Strategy Statistical Appendices (HSSAs).
Note: 'Districts with a Pathfinder' excludes the East Riding of Yorkshire, because only a very small proportion of that district falls within a Pathfinder.

Meanwhile, house prices in many Pathfinder areas, as we have noted, rose substantially. Between 2003-06 rates of growth outstripped other parts of the market (Figure 5.5). Whether this was due to the impact of HMR interventions is a moot point.

Figure 5.5: Annual growth rate in median house sale price (all property types)

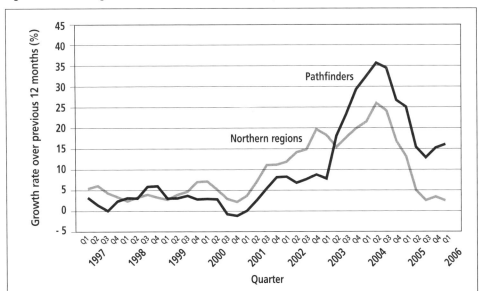

Source: Land Registry; Leather *et al.* (2007).

Refurbishment and demolition may restore confidence to the market, but the addition of fewer than 1,900 new homes – identified in official accounts of Pathfinders (Table 5.4) – will not have altered the underlying trends significantly. The changes may therefore merely reflect a degree of 'catching up' because the cyclical operation of the market means that Northern cities and, within them, lower-price neighbourhoods tend to lag London and the South. Significant price differentials between Pathfinder areas and elsewhere remain (Figure 5.6), and it was the Audit Commission's view that, in relation to prices, 'the available data does not support the view that pathfinder intervention is no longer justified' (Audit Commission, 2006, p.16).

Figure 5.6: Median house sale price (all property types)

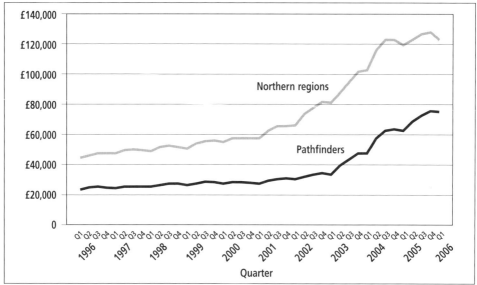

Source: Land Registry; Leather *et al.* (2007).

Measuring success: a question of scale

The ambiguities inherent in interpreting house price signals, as just discussed, highlight the difficulties associated with the evaluation of the HMR programme. At the very least, it is necessary to understand the geography and scale of those price signals. This, in turn, raises questions about the appropriate scale to evaluate the outcomes of market renewal. The Pathfinders are unique entities in that they cover multiple administrative areas (and not just in the way that existing sub-regional partnerships do) and are very large in size. One of the key questions is whether HMR is a national or a neighbourhood policy. That is to say, should HMR's success be measured in terms of the difference it makes at the neighbourhood level within cities, or, is it tackling a wider agenda, one of improving sub-regional economic performance and regional differentials in economies and housing markets? This also raises the question of whether the two objectives are mutually exclusive.

HMR is a significant policy and exhibits many innovative characteristics. Because it was intended to respond to varying market contexts, ODPM established a devolved evaluation structure requiring Pathfinders to be continually self-evaluating, while establishing a 'light touch' national evaluation designed to draw together local evidence to assess the contribution of HMR to national policy objectives. The government's view has always been that HMR would be an evolving policy, able to deal with changes in the market as they occurred, both in response to intervention and in response to other market drivers and shifts in policy. For that reason, it was viewed as an imperative that lessons were to be learned as the Pathfinders went along; responding strategically where necessary at the local level – with policy and funding mechanisms also changing throughout the life of the programme to respond to new challenges.

The overall objective for HMR has been summed up in the *Homes for All* update to the *Communities Plan*: the policy continues in its aim to, *'…eradicate the problems associated with low demand'* by 2020 (ODPM, 2005a). This high level success statement is clearly open to many interpretations. The 'problems', for example, may manifest themselves at a variety of spatial scales, from the neighbourhood to regional and national (e.g., economic competitiveness). The Leunig and Swaffield (2007) paper entitled *Cities Unlimited* highlighted the broader demand issues facing the North, which provocatively challenged the *raison d'être* of parts of the North as essentially manufacturing economies. As we noted in Chapter 1, agendas like the *Northern Way* emphasise the importance of housing responses to these challenges at the supra-regional level, even if the original HMR policy was more focused on localised manifestations of the low-demand problem.

While it remains far too early to gauge the long-term impacts of Housing Market Renewal, there are clear signs from the above analysis that housing market conditions in the affected areas were improving. The extent to which this could be directly attributable to Pathfinder activity is less certain, and it is true that the general direction and speed of the housing market throughout the country during the period 2003-2007 was likely to have had a positive effect on the Pathfinder areas.

In our opening chapter, we noted how the position of New Labour on housing shifted from a concern with social exclusion to a concern with regional competitiveness and how housing contributed to it. The development of the HMR policy reflected this change in emphasis, as it began to plug straight into the strategic apparatus of regional and sub-regional economic growth, and was a key delivery vehicle for performance in the city region development plans (CRDPs). Within these documents, HMR was articulated as a policy delivering objectives for the economy. In other words, *how does housing contribute to the closure of gaps in economic performance?* If this is taken as a measure of success, the Pathfinders' role and impacts will look very different in different contexts. HMR is firmly part of a core competitiveness narrative which justifies the continued investment as a focal point for policy actions to address the lag between built form and economic performance.

Manchester and Newcastle upon Tyne had booming city-regional economies during the first five years of the HMR programme. Clearly, not all of the neighbourhoods in these two cities shared in the benefits of this economic success, but that is a different thing to saying that the housing market is generally weak and is holding the economy back. HMR needs a sharper focus in these areas – connectivity at the neighbourhood scale, perhaps – than it does in, say, East Lancashire or in Stoke on Trent, where the sub-regional economy has been depressed for longer and appears to be in decline at a higher rate than other core cities or HMR areas (see for example, LGA, 2008).

The role of Pathfinders in altering the trajectory of markets is central to their purpose, and whilst evaluating the impact they have had on migration and commuting patterns is difficult, it is possible to draw some general conclusions, especially given the interaction between the role of Pathfinders and the role of deregulated financial markets in delivering large volumes of city centre buy to let housing. In this respect, the impact that Pathfinders have had on the market and creating the conditions for positive migration and commuting patterns is open to debate – especially given the small-scale additions noted above. The buy to let route has possibly contributed to the displacement of investment (which we reflect upon further in the conclusions); but there is also an issue of displacement of opportunity, with a failure to provide the kind of properties needed by families with children and households with above average incomes. The issue of demolition and displacement brings into sharp relief the question of how far the policy of intervention can work, at varying scales to enable aspirations for growth (of economies and populations) on the one hand, and restructuring to engage with existing communities on the other. It also highlights the continual need to consider the competing interests of existing communities and potential new communities that intervention may bring about.

In some areas, there is evidence of positive change, as the net balance of migration reverses, or at least the imbalances become less severe. But, a very resonant note of caution must be rung: the data showing these changes relate to entire local authority areas, and thus include the major city centres that are adjacent to many of the Pathfinder areas (see for example, Leather *et al.*, 2007). The effects of urban renaissance and the residential re-densification of cities over the last decade need to be seen separately from the effects of Housing Market Renewal.

The 2003 *Communities Plan* asserted that, rather than migration from North to South, it was counter-urbanisation that was the main reason for low demand. Whilst it is likely that a combination of weak in-migration, particularly of international migrants, together with counter-urbanisation processes have fuelled low demand, economic decline and its polarising effects, and a previous North-to-South drift in population have set the scene for this. Regardless, the salient point is that all of these processes occur at a wider scale than at the purely local.

Trajectories of decline and recovery

However, whilst spatial scale is important, how to determine what scales are important in what contexts remains unclear. One potential framework for the analysis of the appropriate scale may relate to the historic timing and trajectory of decline in low-demand areas. Not all of the Pathfinders are the same in this respect. Drawing on the Pathfinders' strategic plans and Audit Commission appraisals, Cole and Nevin (2004) have produced a classification of Pathfinders according to their regional economic position and future outlook. One way of developing and formalising this idea would be to examine the trajectory of economic decline, housing market weakness, and any subsequent signs of economic renaissance. For example, it is likely that in such a framework, Manchester-Salford and Merseyside (Liverpool) would be quite far along this trajectory. The deep decline of traditional manufacturing and heavy industry in these areas occurred relatively early and, combined with other forces such as suburbanisation and new extra-urban housing provision, brought about severe market weakness, including private sector abandonment.

Quite a lot has been written in the policy field about 'drivers of change' as they have impacted on urban areas (Cole and Nevin, 2004; Wallace, 2004; also the concept has been extensively adopted in Australia, see for example, DHW, 2001). These drivers have shaped local economies and housing markets and have done so at a variety of spatial scales. The comparatively early decline of land-intensive industrial uses in cities like Manchester, Newcastle upon Tyne and Liverpool posed a significant challenge to the Victorian legacy of mixed land use, where housing areas grew up around major employment sites. Redevelopment of residential areas, such as through slum clearance programmes, used land relatively inefficiently. Considerable slack in land supply permitted the development of major road building programmes in the mid 20th century, which imposed significant environmental disbenefits and divisions upon communities. At the same time, these arterial routes facilitated a rapid expansion of suburban and peripheral developments. The New Towns programme explicitly further decentralised population, in an automotive-driven replication of the mould already set by the railways.

Parts of these areas are beginning an economic recovery based on service sector or cultural industries employment. This is largely a city centre phenomenon and is disconnected from inner city housing and labour markets. Therefore, the natural focus in cities like Manchester may be on communities and neighbourhoods and in making sure that they share the benefits of economic renaissance. In these areas, therefore, it may follow that success (as far as the Pathfinder is concerned) is most appropriately measured at the neighbourhood level.

In some other Pathfinders, for example North Staffordshire, East Lancashire or Hull, further significant job losses and deindustrialisation could still happen. Signs of economic renaissance remain elusive. The issue might be better expressed as whether a weak housing market (low values, poor quality, and a lack of choice for upwardly-mobile households), is holding back chances of economic recovery, or, the ushering in of new economic modes. Success in these areas is most appropriately measured at the sub-regional level. If this is the case, then it is likely that the Northern Way provides the most appropriate framework in which HMR policy sits.

However, there are potentially two problems with this. First, as we have seen, the economic unlocking arguments are not shared by, nor necessarily appropriate for, all of the Pathfinders. Second, as the Northern Way itself recognises, not all of the affected areas of market weakness are covered by Pathfinders, and there is also the issue of new housing provision outside the Pathfinders. These require a strategic regional (and extra-regional) planning response, which Integrated Regional Strategies (IRS) are expected to take up. How the Pathfinders engage with the IRS process is likely to be an important determinant of their success.

Changing objectives

Changes in emphasis and focus on HMR policy have been detectable throughout its short life to date and have affected its evaluation. There has been a distinct shift away from it being a policy that was explicitly concerned with a very visible, neighbourhood manifestation of the problem. Thus, the type of blight and abandonment that Power and Mumford (1999) graphically singled out has been generally accepted to have been the exception rather than the rule. What has been vexing policy-makers since then is the pervasive comparative weakness of some local housing markets and, in particular, the parallel economic disparities at neighbourhood level (and wider). There is now arguably more of an emphasis on the connectivity of people and place; people to jobs; and places with each other.

Taking various sources, from the National Housing Federation's original submission to the Treasury's comprehensive spending review (Nevin, 2001) to the *Communities Plan* and *Homes for All*, it is possible to observe how far Pathfinder objectives have evolved in relation to changing circumstances. They have matured from a focus on a limited range of outcomes to a wider set of outcomes, and to incorporate a number of process objectives. The NHF spending review submission made the case for housing market renewal as a process for restructuring cities, but the original issue which brought about the Pathfinder programme was the more readily visible problem of low demand, as characterised by empty and abandoned properties and low property values, highlighted dramatically by the 2002 Select Committee report into empty homes (HC 240-I, 2001-02). Subsequent events, notably rising house prices and increasing demand for social rented housing, combined with the maturing of the programme, have ensured that the question of low demand *per se* is much less evident in *Homes for All*, which characterised the Pathfinder programme as being concerned with, '...*tackling failing housing markets, creating places where people will wish to live, addressing relative price differentials, breaking up concentrations of deprivation'* and *'creating mixed communities'*. In addition, a range of process issues have emerged on the agenda including the alignment of investment strategies, formation of partnerships and attraction of private investment. Table 5.6 attempts to demonstrate some of the objectives that have been explicitly associated with HMR and comments on how these have changed.

Table 5.6: Objectives associated with HMR

Topic area	Examples of objectives that have been associated with the HMR programme
Tackling problems associated with low demand	• Tackling low demand • Eradicating problems caused by low demand (by 2020) • Tackling abandonment • Tackling dereliction • Tackling empty homes
Achieving the physical regeneration of housing	• Replacing obsolete housing • Eliminating the 'worst' housing • Refurbishing housing • Creating new housing • Creating a wider choice of properties • Achieving high quality design • Using the opportunities created by heritage
Improving markets	• Understanding what drives the housing market • Closing the gap between Pathfinder areas and elsewhere in terms of vacancies and house values by one third (by 2010) • Creating a balanced market • Facing up to decline • Managing change • Addressing affordability problems where they occur in Pathfinder areas
Sustainability	• Recreating sustainable communities in low-demand areas • Creating cohesion within the community • Halting or reversing the exodus of residents • Creating mixed communities • Creating identity, image and culture to be proud of
Connectedness/ integration	• Connecting HMR programmes to other regeneration and economic development activities • Securing good quality, focused public sector services and physical/social/economic environments • Consulting local people • Residents to see things change for the better • Tackling deprivation

A number of themes emerge from the analysis presented in Table 5.6. The core aims of the programme have remained largely unaltered. However, what is understood as constituting 'the problem' of low demand has shifted perceptibly. Tackling low demand remains the core objective of the programme as confirmed by *Homes for All*. An official definition of 'low demand' exists,[7] although this is open to interpretation and some components are difficult to measure. In particular, more recent focus has been on the problems 'caused by' low demand, although this is not elaborated upon. Tackling abandonment and dereliction were originally high profile objectives, but are now much less commonly referred to; while the problem of empty homes remains a high priority, this is seen as a broader problem not always directly connected to low demand.

In terms of HMR as a programme for achieving physical regeneration of housing, a wider concern with obsolescence has arguably replaced a more narrow focus on demolishing the 'worst' housing. Together with other activities (refurbishment and new provision) demolition is now seen as part of a series of means by which to achieve other market renewal objectives. In particular, concerns about the need to preserve the built heritage have become much more prominent. Objectives that have remained the same throughout the programme include a focus on design quality and the use of the housing stock to create more choice for households.

The improvement of housing markets lies at the heart of the HMR approach. The distinction between a 'well functioning market' (which may only be one that 'clears' in a classical economic sense), and a 'balanced market' (which will enable wider objectives), is brought out. A market that clears will be one that finds a buyer for all housing, regardless of the price or the ultimate use of the property, which may include it being left empty. Specific objectives that contribute to market balance, on the other hand, might specify an optimal social use for property, or might seek to measure the gaps in market outcomes (such as house prices and vacancies) between HMR areas and elsewhere. However, it is probably the case that while these specific objectives have gained in prominence, the wider concept of balance is not rigorously measured. 'Tough talking' language (such as 'facing up to decline'), which was about recognising the loss of economic functions, has ceded to more process-oriented objectives about managing change and the transition from old to new economic modes and functions. Affordability was a later but very significant addition to the range of HMR concerns. It was not a prominent feature of early debates, but it is now important both in terms of public appetite for the programme and the costs of delivering it.

Sustainability has the attraction of being a problem-independent solution that transcends both low-demand and high-demand contexts. It is obviously central to the

---

7 This is the same as the definition used for the annual statistical returns made by all English local authorities to central government.

government's approach to housing, and an official definition exists,[8] although measurement is more difficult. Some detractors have claimed that the focus on sustainability (including the sustainability of growth), has diverted attention away from the need to regenerate urban areas (Urban Task Force, 2005). In some (but not all) areas, there is an explicit concern with community cohesion, including the importance of race relations and desegregation. A concern about population flows was an explicit objective of the programme from the early stages, although – as we noted earlier – while the early focus was on national flows (e.g., North to South), a more subtle, sub-regional interpretation centred around counter-urbanisation has gained prominence. The role of mixed communities in delivering sustainability now features strongly, although there has been less made about an initial focus on local identities and images. This could suggest that Pathfinders are explicitly planning for new population groups rather than existing residents.

It is now recognised that intervention in the housing stock will not on its own achieve the wider objectives of the programme, so the importance of processes that ensure that HMR is aligned with wider strategies (such as *The Northern Way*) has increased in prominence and importance. These include economic, transport, planning, health and crime strategies as well as programmes for tackling the environment and deprivation. Specific process objectives about consultation are now more prominent, although there remains a recognition of the time it might take for improvements to work through and the potential for some areas to worsen before improvements are apparent, especially where demolition is planned. There have also consistently been references to the objectives of tackling deprivation – mainly because poor areas are normally, but not always, ones of housing market weakness. Generally, however, HMR looks to the fostering of links with other programmes (such as the Working Neighbourhoods Fund) to further this objective.

Summary

This chapter has looked at the impact of HMR to date. Recent changes in the direction of HMR policy, and its wider policy context, finds that while there is an inherent tension between neighbourhood and regional/national objectives, there are a number of reasons why the 'economic arguments' for HMR are likely to increase in importance. These can still be measured both at the neighbourhood and sub-regional levels, although different 'trajectories of decline', and sub-regional economic situations among Pathfinders will determine the appropriate scale at which to measure success.

HMR policy may miss a trick if it reverts to more traditional forms of housing and neighbourhood renewal. Evidence of price rises and worsening affordability prior to

---

8 *Homes for All* (ODPM, 2005a) has a short definition and a long definition of a sustainable community. The short definition is: '...*places where people want to live and work, now and in the future*'.

the credit crunch were superficially worrying, but did not mean that the problem of low demand was miraculously solved. Coincident with price rises has been widening house price polarisation and increasing evidence that local housing markets and local communities are becoming 'disconnected'. The burgeoning investment role of housing bolstered the second homes and buy to let markets and will continue to do so. House prices are likely to be increasingly driven by national macro-economic conditions including their competitiveness against other forms of investment.

The vagaries of the housing market continue to challenge HMR both philosophically and practically as a programme: can a government policy ever be sufficiently clued-up about the market to make effective interventions? Are not the concepts of the 'market' and of 'intervention' forever doomed to lead parallel and unco-operative lives? If average house prices were rising everywhere before the credit crunch – including some of the sharpest rises being in Pathfinder areas – was the market itself not solving the 'problem' of its own accord?

The ultimate evaluation of a policy like HMR clearly needs to tread carefully. In many ways there are interesting aspects of policy to explore. While many of these may have a relevance that is unique to the English housing market and housing system, the philosophical underpinnings of market renewal and its relationship to wider markets are of international relevance and interest. Before making any evaluative judgements, the reader needs to be cognisant of both its objectives and its concerns for the links between housing and other markets. At the same time, it must be borne in mind that HMR is a uniquely devolved programme. Despite more recent attempts to rein back control of the programme to the centre, it remains a policy that is steered by a very small team at central government level, and which has always insisted only on a relatively 'light touch' in terms of performance management and evaluation (especially in comparison to, say, New Deal for Communities).

The intervention areas represent a significant shift from previous area-based regeneration initiatives. As was seen in earlier chapters, the Pathfinders cover areas that are very large indeed – ranging in population from approximately 150,000 to 300,000 inhabitants (see Table 4.1). They were designed explicitly to cover multiple local authority areas and their boundaries were intended to reflect housing markets rather than the convenience of administrative geography.

Whether the philosophy of market renewal is the right one and Pathfinders' implementation of market renewal fits the spirit of that philosophy are important and enduring questions. Immediately following the 2005 general election, *The Guardian* (11 May 2005) reported that the future of HMR was to be one of the first items in the 'in-tray' of the then-incoming minister for communities and local government, David Miliband. HMR survived this first real 'test'. A Treasury spending review in 2007, led by a new ministerial team, looked less certain given that the programme had lost one of its departmental champions in John Prescott. However, again the programme was retained and in 2009, further funds were committed by central government, an apparent testament to the importance of the programme in delivering new housing growth – itself a key political and public service commitment of the Brown government. Questions, however, as to how HMR will contribute to government targets for housing and neighbourhoods are likely to remain on the agenda for some time and in the post-credit crunch environment, the political arguments can be tilted towards an early exit strategy, or maintaining a supply-side focus within the Pathfinders and associated growth points.

Finally, and most importantly, it appears that one of the main issues is that of spatial scale. The relationship between housing and labour markets – and hence the relationship between economic growth and housing markets, is particularly dependent on scale. In those Pathfinders where this is an attendant pressure (politically or otherwise), local measures of HMR 'success' will naturally look very different than in Pathfinders which have more local aspirations of neighbourhood connectivity. The way that HMR is able to find a niche between the regional structures developed by New Labour and a growing 'localism' agenda will be critical to its future successes.

CHAPTER 6:
Retrospect and prospect: delivering sustainable and resilient housing markets

Introduction

As we noted in Chapter 1, concern with the 'socially excluded' became one of the defining characteristics of early New Labour. Urban blight and poor housing conditions – hand in hand with social problems – helped to define New Labour's domestic policy focus. This transformational agenda – not only of society, but of its housing and urban space – led directly to a variety of policies and programmes such as urban renaissance (Urban Task Force, 1999), decent homes (DETR, 2000b), the National Strategy for Neighbourhood Renewal (SEU, 2001) and ultimately, Housing Market Renewal (ODPM, 2003). HMR in particular, has signalled both an acceptance of the dominance of the market in housing provision as well as a will to intervene in its operations where necessary.

Housing Market Renewal was presented as a tool for re-calibrating low-demand areas to the needs of a competitive economy. The competitiveness agenda overtook the 'social exclusion' agenda and was underpinned by narratives around the 'knowledge' and 'creative' economy. Rescaling arguments were presented to support and underpin these narratives concerning the competitiveness of regions and city regions, and the need to attract and retain the right kind of workforce for a knowledge-based economy (KBE) and creative economy to prosper. Creating good quality neighbourhoods in the Pathfinder areas was paramount to this agenda. The prelude to HMR had stressed the need for housing pathways, and re-aligning the housing market and the evidence base of HMR emphasised the asymmetry between the housing and labour markets, by presenting evidence that showed the failure to provide housing pathways for aspirational groups. In this context, the Housing Market Renewal 'mindset' engaged with the 'core' narrative of competitiveness by asking, 'how does housing fit within the competitive economy?'. Through demolition and replacement, HMR, therefore, introduced a tension between existing communities and a new set of households with different aspirations and tastes.

The last fifteen years (1995-2010) has witnessed unusual volatility in the housing market and has been characterised by three distinct phases: i) a period which combined high rates of abandonment, falling waiting lists for social housing and rapid rates of churning and turnover in the rented sector in the North and Midlands (1995-2003); ii) a period of record increases in house prices and problems of housing supply and affordability (2003-2007), and iii) a period of almost universal devaluation in the market, fuelled by the restriction in the supply of credit, the concomitant collapse in the number of housing mortgage products, and a stalled supply pipeline as builders and developers struggled with the reduced supply of credit to fund their activities (2007-2010). The unparalleled slump in the market has led to house prices falling by more than 20 per cent and economists predicting that values will fall further (*The Guardian*, 2009). In some markets, such as city centre flats, market confidence has been decimated as prices have dropped by more than half in some cases. A special report in investment trends in UK cities reported on flats selling for £50,000 less than the owner had originally pad over an 18 month period and repossessed flats being dumped on the market at much reduced prices (*The Guardian*, 2008). The report gives examples of market prices deflation such as a one-bedroom flat sold by a developer for £140,000 in 2001 fetching just £87,970 in 2008, and a two-bed flat selling for £180,000 in 2005 achieiving just £128,000. The price falls of between 28-38 per cent are not reflected in an overall decline in UK house prices, but reflect a differentiated market and the over-inflated prices achieved through a distributed network of arms length investors encouraged by a deregulated financial system.

In this book we have used the experience of the Housing Market Renewal programme as a means for exploring changes in perspectives and interventions in the housing market, and to explore whether this has worked. The HMR programme was the result of a new set of perspectives on housing. Housing was increasingly seen not just as a locus of processes of social exclusion and a reflection of those processes, but also central in shaping the links between local areas and regional economies. These twin perspectives were emblematic of policy developments associated with New Labour and a shift towards a competitiveness agenda which viewed housing as a vital component of the development of a modern economy.

The challenge facing the market beyond 2010 is of a different magnitude from the late 1990s and arises from a different set of starting points and drivers. The credit crunch and resultant recession is a global phenomenon affecting most markets whereas the problems of low and changing demand was very localised in the UK. The credit crunch and recent housing market downturn resulted from excessive supply of credit rather than the lagged housing market response to industrial restructuring and adjustments in the demand for social housing, which was the case with low demand. As we saw in Chapter 2, in the case of Liverpool the drivers were operating at a variety of spatial and temporal scales and were dependent on previous policy eras, for example, i) decentralisation of planning during the 1950s and 1960s; ii) diversification of the economy during the 1970s and 1980s; iii) the impact of national welfare policies in the 1980s and 1990s; iv) the reinvention of housing markets (e.g. student markets) during the post-war period; and v) the fragmented governance and political instability of the early 1980s. The evidence base was slow to catch up with what local authorities knew was happening 'on the ground', but it gathered pace quickly and support for intervention grew quickly because of speed at which political alignments and coalitions were being formed. None of the subsequent phase of policy development had the foresight to predict the dramatic collapse witnessed since 2007; partly because of the speed of reaction and implementation of policies designed to arrest what had been a slow, long-run of decline.

A great deal of emphasis in this book has been on the asymmetry of housing and labour markets. The credit crunch has demonstrated the degree to which our evidence and foresight has been limited in its ability to forewarn policy-makers of the consequences and impact of different economic scenarios and potential outcomes. The post-credit crunch and the recession question our ability to deliver sustainable housing markets. The combined evidence base of HMR could not predict the credit crunch and subsequent housing market failure. HMR interventions were designed to underpin the housing and economic renaissance of the North and Midlands and failed to avert or arrest a collapse in prices and demand. Given this state of affairs, what confidence do we have in the future development of research and policy in housing market behaviour? What does this mean for a policy agenda in building sustainable housing markets? Given the global interconnectedness and spatial scale at which processes are operating, can a regional or national response insulate future policy from negative effects?

The goal of this book has been to consider such questions alongside the policy developments in housing markets over the past decade or so. The question therefore arises as to how we can avoid such fluctuations and market volatility in the future? How can we build sustainability and resilience into the housing market so that we can avoid the repetition of excessive fluctuations in the market? In this concluding chapter we consider the lessons learnt from the low and changing demand debate, the implementation and adaptation of HMR policy and the prospects for the future especially in the context of the post-credit crunch challenges. The requirement is for a 'new normal' for housing-led regeneration and renewal ('Redesign our Regeneration', Tim Williams, *Regeneration & Renewal*, 11 January 2010), and the increasing importance of building in resilience to public policy-making and the strategic housing function. In the following sections we reflect on some of the problems that beset and continue to challenge HMR as a housing policy programme and consider what needs to change in order to deliver more sustainable and resilient housing markets in the future.

The rhetoric of low demand: the ambition of HMR

In the context of recent growth in the housing market – including growth in previously low-demand Housing Market Renewal areas – it is easy to forget how significant the experience of 'low demand' was. In the early 2000s, after about five years of general acceptance of the existence of low demand, weak local housing markets and empty homes were still posing very difficult questions for policy-makers especially for those planning, developing and managing social housing; it was also having severe implications for those who owned their own homes, or, were tenants and residents in affected communities. Low house prices in the worst affected low-demand areas impacted on social and residential mobility by trapping homeowners in low-value housing in their neighbourhoods in a spiral of decline. Images of boarded up housing in Merseyside and other deindustrialised conurbations highlighted the polarised nature of the market in the late 1990s and the plight of many of those trapped in low-value housing – so we should guard against delusion and not overlook the plight of homeowners and tenants in such neighbourhoods – their interests need to be protected as well as those of future households. By the mid 2000s house prices had moved so dramatically and the situation had changed so completely that the issue for housing policy and housing markets was now one of 'getting into the market', rather than 'getting on in the market'.

The distinction between low demand as a 'real' market condition with real losers and a drag on economic performance and neighbourhood approval, and low demand as a general narrative of the North and Midlands (low-demand areas in their own right), highlights how low demand could exist as a phenomenon which engendered a set of behaviours and responses among actors in the housing arena. It quickly became a much abused, catch-all term for unpopular housing and reflected the way the housing policy world was shocked by the way low demand appeared to manifest itself very quickly. It is not an over-exaggeration to say that low demand became the predominant housing concern towards the end of the 1990s. Low demand became firmly embedded within the housing lexicon and continues to be used interchangeably to refer to lettings difficulties, high void rates and turnover, investment 'mistakes' and as a characteristic of regional housing market differences. A mindset of low demand extended to a general pessimism about social housing and its role; and certain neighbourhoods and their role. The repercussions of this were a quickly growing concern with alternative modes of investment and its delivery, remodelling the form and extent of housing supply and the opening up of questions of demolition – a discussion that had always been previously somewhat taboo following slum clearance in the 1960s. But, because low demand and abandonment in some parts of the North and Midlands were so stark, the evidence was used to suggest a significant threat or risk to a much wider area. In retrospect, it is easy to detect a rhetoric that fuelled the ambition of HMR. The rhetoric was used to exaggerate and gain political traction.

Perhaps because of this, the HMR programme was set with an over-ambitious set of objectives: for example, in addressing low demand it was set with the aim of reducing the house price differential and the gap in prices between areas. A key moment in the genesis of HMR was the select committee inquiry into the problem of empty homes. This made some strong recommendations and was quite unflinching in its description of what would happen without a market renewal approach. The committee talked of northern cities being wholly and unremittingly comprised of *'...a devastated no-man's land encompassed...by suburbia'* (HC 240-I) unless remedial action was taken. The enormous cost and time implications of what was being proposed were clearly acknowledged, as was the futility of any intervention that did not involve co-ordinated policy and leadership across a wide area. It made the case for sweeping away the past and was consistent with a Blairite modernisation agenda. It was framed in a way that suggested a total collapse in some parts of the North, and that HMR represented a once-in-a-lifetime chance to develop a new and modern future for the North's cities:

> ...*the problem of market collapse is also a unique opportunity. It gives us the chance to restructure and rebuild our cities for the twenty-first century. We must now seize that opportunity* (Great Britain, 2002, p.5).

> [HMR is] *absolutely the last chance to get what we call regeneration right in the UK* (Brendan Nevin on *File on Four*, 'Urban Regeneration' on BBC Radio 4 on 8 March 2005).

However, this was patently not true. To claim that HMR was a last chance to get regeneration right highlighted the degree of rhetoric that beset the programme, and undermined its long-term credibility.

Oddly enough, given New Labour's concerns with communitarianism in other strands of its urban policy (Imrie and Raco, 2003), HMR could be characterised as representing a new form of a rather old-fashioned concept. It was centrally designated (without the competitive bidding associated with the era of City Challenge and the Single Regeneration Budget), and had significant powers and an array of policy options. Curiously for a programme that had its powers drawn quite widely, community consultation mechanisms were not as well developed from the outset, as they perhaps ought to have been (Cole and Flint, 2007). The ambition and rhetoric of the programme created confusion as to how precise interventions would bring about the perceived improvements in the market, which in turn confused the degree to which HMR was accountable, and how Pathfinders should consult. HMR should have developed more effective accountability from the start and could have better anticipated need for effective community engagement (Cole and Flint, 2007). The programme had echoes of post-war comprehensive redevelopment programmes which were also characterised by similar sorts of central-local relations (Jones and Evans, 2006, p.1493). Demolition and clearance attracted considerable criticism, with some detractors likening it to post-war slum clearance and replacement with systems-built housing (Save Britain's Heritage, 2006), and trenchant criticisms of HMR, both from a pragmatic perspective and also from the point of view of the alleged subjugation of residents' views in the face of professional 'power elites' (Allen, 2008).

HMR presented and continues to present a paradoxical set of policies for sustainable communities by backing a programme of market renewal that was using demolition as one of its main tools. An irreconcilable 'knot' in reasoning had been reached: tackling poor neighbourhoods and housing conditions may do little to fundamentally restructure the market but will achieve some short-term, local-level 'wins'. But, it is unlikely to have a significant impact on long-term market stability and the closure of sub-regional economic differentials. In part, achieving the latter needed a highly effective exercise in consultation (or public relations at the least). At the very minimum, Pathfinders needed to be very clear in their own minds as to the strategic aims and objectives of their intervention and to communicate this more effectively. However, the question always remains with clearance as to whether it is possible to convince local residents, many of whom will have invested significant time and resources in their own house that demolition will be in the interests of some 'greater good'? It is a question of *place leadership* (see later in this chapter). More practically, appropriate relocation and compensation policies needed to be developed; as we noted, the rapid change in house prices quickly undermined this and also made the programme prohibitively expensive.

The HMR baseline evaluation report (Leather *et al.*, 2007) found that a number of Pathfinders were giving renewed emphasis to community engagement, employing community development or media relations consultants. The evaluation's authors acknowledged that such initiatives would take some time to bed in and to enable trust to develop. But some of the Pathfinders were also having to grapple with complex ethnic and religious tensions within their areas, in addition to reconciling support for existing long-standing residents (many of whom are living in circumstances of social deprivation), and attracting new households. It was the failure of the programme to engage more holistically with stakeholders that created the atmosphere of cynicism and hostility to the programme, and as we noted in Chapter 5, the heritage lobby combined with local community campaigns to provide strong opposition to demolition and clearance plans, which were then subsequently reduced by CLG.

Measuring success

The policy of clearance and failure to consult properly on this early on, dogged the programme, therefore, a key evaluative question to consider is whether HMR was the right policy design to deliver sustainability and address both the competitiveness of declining neighbourhoods and weak markets, whilst at the same time protecting social inclusion? The criticisms of HMR suggest that it had shifted emphasis and lost sight of a social inclusion agenda. Moreover, during the period 2004-2007, the market appeared to have solved the problem of low prices and excessive abandonment and the emphasis of housing policy and politics of housing shifted to the problems of supply and affordability.

In many senses, the question posed by HMR was the right one; it challenged politicians and policy-makers to do something about this, and it created a spatial focus for intervention (Pathfinders), in some of the most problematic and intractable housing markets and neighbourhoods in England. It also challenged the growing division between neighbourhoods and the emerging economy – what we have described in Chapter 2 as the *asymmetry* between housing and labour markets – and the *path dependency* (how previous eras of economic development and housing policy lock areas into particular development trajectories) of these neighbourhoods.[9] Therefore, despite the rise in prices and the subsequent credit crunch, the Pathfinder areas will likely remain weak markets, since within a market system the differentials between areas will remain reasonably constant over long periods. By maintaining a consistent long-term focus on these weak markets, and by sequencing planning and housing market investments into these areas, then long-term sustainability may be secured. But, the amount of time that has elapsed since the start of the programme is too short for us to be definitive about its success. The path dependency of space, the haste by which the programme was drawn together, its over ambitious nature, and the criticisms that continue to attract negative attention to the programme, remain fundamental challenges to its success.

The backlash and criticism towards HMR highlighted the contradiction and tension between a competitiveness and inclusion agenda which served to confuse the goals and objectives of HMR. The core 'narrative' (around the knowledge-based economy, creative cities and competitiveness) had the effect of driving out other voices and perspectives. It was possibly part of the reason for a backlash against the Housing Market Renewal concept which resulted in critiques and resistance by communities affected by clearance. The perception was one of gentrification or state-sponsored social engineering and accusations of a revanchist state. These are fundamental issues of *displacement*, i.e., that the demolition and clearance was designed to displace existing residents and appealed to a new set of (middle-class) households outside the area. What needed to be emphasised was that the improvements were also intended to benefit leavers – households that were moving out of low-demand areas because they did not have a housing pathway or option to stay, could not find the right housing for their needs, or were concerned about the value of any future investment.

Financial deregulation as a mechanism of displacement

Sensitivities towards policies of displacement need to be widened to understand how the general market conditions were shaping to displace alternative outcomes for Pathfinder areas. Pathfinder areas have been systematically undermined by countervailing pressures that have effectively redistributed empty and dysfunctional

---

9 We have already noted that evidence on deprivation shows that the pattern of relative deprivation at small area level has not altered significantly over the past 20 years, indicating a high degree of *path dependency* for some neighbourhoods (Lee and Ferrari, 2007); associated with this, patterns of housing investment have tended to reinforce the underpinning economic and social function of neighbourhoods with a strong pattern of low-value housing built in low-value areas demonstrated by recent research (Bramley *et al.*, 2007).

housing stock, and the seeds of a potentially new 'low demand' through the over-supply of monolithic housing represented by city centre apartments. Investment in city centre flats/city living in areas adjacent to core Pathfinder areas underpinned a 'knowledge' economy narrative and fitted with a logic of creating markets for different 'segments' of the economy.

Patterns of activity and investment that went on within and adjacent to HMR areas, but not funded by HMR, have therefore arguably had more influence on market outcomes than has HMR itself over the past decade (see Chapter 5). Some of this activity displaced investment and renewal work in Pathfinder areas and contributed to an over-extension of the market. As we have seen with the credit crunch, the over-extension of 'effective demand' contributed to a wholesale collapse in lender and purchaser confidence. Over the decade to 2007, a number of factors aligned which allowed the development of city living and city centre apartment development, and was triggered by a number of key decisions and market assumptions:

- The planning system's emphasis on greater density (how many units?) as opposed to utilisation (*who* will use them and *how* effectively?) which was underpinned by Lord Rogers' Urban Task Force in 1999.
- Assumptions that volume and smaller dwelling sizes were required following the influence of Alan Holmans' housing projections and assumptions about household formation and household size (Holmans, 2001).
- An explosive growth in the buy to let industry fuelled by a highly deregulated financial sector and a relaxation by the banks on the rules concerning equity leverage.

These features of the housing and planning system and the wider economy aligned to result in the delivery of an excessive amount of housing that was not 'needed', but was 'expressed' demand by 'off-plan' investors. Economic prosperity and increased equity (through increased share of outright ownership), had increased the potential for investment and a growing number of outright homeowners used their equity to purchase stakes of communities at arms' length. This displaced private sector investment in HMR and the renewal of Pathfinder suburbs which would have linked to existing services and expressed 'need'. This also had the effect of diluting direct ownership and 'community interest' in new developments in city centre locations.

Competitiveness, knowledge and financial models combined to confuse the 'expressed' needs and demand within local housing markets. The credit crunch has demonstrated the need for a new model of economic development and housing-led regeneration, which recognises the tensions between need and 'effective' demand, and acts as a bulwark to the abstracted notion of *competitiveness* and housing's role within it. What has been lost in these abstract narratives is that, first and foremost, housing should be seen as shelter. The credit crunch has provided a definitive answer that the supply of credit is finite and could not carry on forever. Its seemingly relentless supply created a dissonance between investment and underlying needs. This can be witnessed in the high proportion of empty flats now evidenced in cities such as Birmingham, Leicester, Manchester and Leeds, which are surrounded by high concentrations of ethnic minorities in overcrowded and deprived housing conditions. The post-credit crunch/low-demand era signals the need for the development of new models of housing-led regeneration which are community-based and where there is the potential for leverage, reinvestment and equity redistribution built into the 'model'. It requires the protection of communities from excessive speculative building and investment from arms' length investors. It also requires the sequencing of investment to be regulated in order to protect low-demand areas and Pathfinders that are vulnerable to long-term structural weakness.

Changing objectives: a strength or weakness of HMR?

Even over the course of its short life, HMR has seen a shift in its objectives. Originally, a clear descendent of an early-New Labour focus on renewal in housing policy, it began to occupy a much less comfortable place, struggling to reconcile the new dominant discourse of 'supply', with its local tactical programmes of clearance, reconstruction and new build. HMR was also undermined by a rising housing market and a 'growth' agenda which partly deflected activity away from HMR areas. As house prices rose and affordability problems dominated the housing agenda, this allowed ministers to put pressure on HMR to deliver on emerging political agendas such as 'growth' and 'Respect' and to re-orientate the policy and the programme to fit concerns about affordability. The programme thus became focused on 'supply' rather than 'restructuring' and housing policy changed in its language and focus. The concern with renewal receded, to be replaced by a more prevalent discourse on 'growth' (Growth Areas, New Growth Points) and culminating in a housing green paper (CLG, 2007a), with its focus on increasing the supply of new housing. The Brown government's aspiration to provide an additional three million homes by 2020, represented a significant increase over and above already-contentious house building targets, and was accompanied by some 'hard talk' from the department of Communities and Local Government (CLG) in terms of building on flood-plains and questioning the sanctity of green belt land.

In the late 1990s, it would not have seemed unreasonable to use house prices as a mechanism of measuring HMR interventions and how successful they were in re-calibrating housing and labour markets. But, as the supply of credit and explosion of investment opportunities created false optimism, house prices as measures of success proved controversial, and this controversy was only alerted to policy-makers when affordability levels became intolerable, and became political when the policy of demolition appeared anathema in such a heated and seemingly under-supplied housing market.

The goals and measurement of future housing market performance and renewal need to change. The goal of HMR was to re-align the housing market with the economy. Whilst competitiveness is measured at regional and sub-regional level in terms of productivity and gross value added (GVA), housing market performance relied on too simple a set of measures which did not relate to the structural problems. The programme was essentially set up on the basis of three indicators: empty properties, house prices and waiting lists ('low demand'). In terms of prices, it was tasked with reducing the differential in prices between the Pathfinders and the regional average.

During the period of house price growth (2003-07), policy-makers and commentators found it much more difficult to refer to the problem of low demand. This underscores the sway that house prices hold over the overall analysis of housing market conditions. The implication is that if prices are rising then everything must be fine – or at least that the problems were yesterday's concern. Yet, an over-reliance on house prices as an indicator of overall market 'health' might also lead us to some spectacularly wrong conclusions. There might be the temptation to view the problem of low demand as simply a mis-specification of some other problem. What was really happening might not have been fundamental and structural, but simply 'more of the same': residualisation in the social rented sector; poor private sector stock condition; low incomes and unpopular areas. Weak local economies and unemployment may have compounded this, but the situation may have ultimately been revocable without major intervention as the economy recovered. A focus on house prices would most certainly support this conclusion.

However, a focus on rising house prices also potentially involves missing the 'real story' about housing markets. This real story might suggest that house price growth will do little to solve any of the fundamental problems in the long term. Whilst prices rose, problems of widening spatial and sectoral differences in the market did not go away; they were merely masked by the optimistic biases provided by house price headlines. Average house prices do little to explain the variety of properties bought and sold; and the top end of the market has a tendency to disproportionately drive the average. Mean (average) house prices are consistently above the median price in most analyses. In addition, house prices only relate to properties that sell and do not necessarily say anything about the wider structure of the housing stock, or of household needs for the thousands of households that do not move in any given year. This is particularly relevant for the social rented sector, where John Hills' review of the sector reminds us of the problems of immobile households and worklessness among social tenants.[10]

---

10 Hills (2007) also cites evidence from Sefton (forthcoming) which suggests that only 0.5 per cent of social tenants finding work moved long distance to do so, compared to 1.0 per cent of owners and 4.1 per cent of private renters.

It certainly seems to stretch credibility to suggest that the severe structural weaknesses that were identified in the last decade had been solved of their own accord and without intervention over the course of three or four years. Alan Murie has consistently suggested that it is not absolute low demand that is of sole concern, but problems associated with the changing nature of demand (Lee and Murie, 2002). His analytical framework allows problems that are the reverse of the 'classic' symptoms of low demand (such as affordability problems), to be reconciled within a consistent market framework. Hence, indicators of the market (such as prices or turnover rates), may mean different things in different contexts. The term 'changing demand' also better reflects the fact that needs and aspirations continue to change over time, partly in response to changes in the way that individuals organise their lives and where they choose to live.

House price growth does not necessarily mean that demand is consistent throughout the housing market, nor is it sensitive to how the form of that demand may have changed: an increase in speculative investment activity (buy to let), and multiple property ownership, are key examples of how this might have changed. This forces us to consider whether these wider forms of demand represent an efficient or acceptable outcome in housing policy terms. Markets continually have to deal with fluctuations in both the schedules of supply and demand and the market for housing in this respect is no different. The problems associated with low-demand conditions (neighbourhood unpopularity; social exclusion; poor stock condition) are persistent, are not being cleared by the market, and co-exist with general market confidence in other contexts and locales. This re-emphasises the need to focus on changing demand, thereby building resilience into the strategic function of planning and housing.

House price change therefore dominated and became a fixation of policy and a measure of success. The next phase of policy development for housing and urban renewal and the monitoring and evaluation of such policies needs to be driven by a different set of measures of success and outcomes; these should include:

- Measurement of spatial outcomes which captures the *utilisation* of housing and land as opposed to the *density* of buildings.
- How house prices are influenced by investment decisions – who owns what, and what share of investments is from outside the region or strategic housing market area, leaving it vulnerable to credit supply whilst distorting the relationship between local labour markets and housing costs.
- The economy and wellbeing of the local community need to be balanced – for example, the GVA and GDP measures of economic success and competitiveness need to be assessed alongside alternative measures of social and economic wellbeing, such as the Index of Sustainable Economic Welfare (ISEW).

More qualitative dimensions of success therefore need to be incorporated into the evaluation of housing led renewal. HMR, and its successor policies, need to deliver neighbourhoods with higher quality housing that balances need and is cautious of 'expressed demand' in the market. The strategies of individual HMR Pathfinders will probably need to be much more responsive to local differences than they have been to date. Whilst many of the symptoms look the same, it is clear that some of the causes of the problem in the bigger, resurgent cities are different to those in the poorly-connected, economically-depressed sub-regions.

Data management

Of course, the emphasis on house prices was also partly due to the explosion of IT and data availability. Housing Market Renewal represented a significant leap in the 'spatial literacy' of local authorities and the ability to share intelligence across local authority boundaries and, more importantly, to begin to create a shared perspective on the dynamics and trajectories of neighbourhoods and housing markets. In our introduction we refer to the rather myopic view of housing and its contribution to social disadvantage that New Labour inherited. The 'worst estates' was symptomatic of a central view of local authority responsibilities towards 'the poor', which emphasised the symptom rather than the underlying structural and spatial causes. HMR provided the impetus to unleash the collective data and understanding and bring that to bear in a unified and largely coherent way within the focal point of Pathfinder boundaries.

The evidence presented by the prospectuses indicates that the analysis of the housing market in each of the Pathfinders does not represent a precise science with a core set of common indicators and a developed methodology for determining the nature of the housing market. As we have emphasised in the introduction, the analysis of the housing market represents the intersection of a number of disciplinary areas. The asymmetry between housing and labour markets and the time lags between them means that local features of the housing market and its operation locally will differ from place to place. The original HMR prospectuses demonstrate how a combination of drivers and individual commentaries were used to look at the intersection between the processes most likely to affect changing and future trajectories of demand. In utilising a range of evidence, the Pathfinders sometimes presented this at an aggregate level supplemented with more detailed analysis in appendices. The drivers of the housing market were often treated summarily in the initial Pathfinder prospectuses; however, this concealed a large amount of intelligence gathering and bespoke commissioning of research, or built on pre-existing housing market analysis of low and changing demand. All of the prospectuses generally referred to the 'areas at risk' analysis developed by CURS, which was a central component of the evidence base informing the selection of the Pathfinder areas and the definition of their precise boundaries.

The capacity for innovation and local flexibility was therefore recognised explicitly from the outset of the policy and was responsible for unleashing much creativity and local variation in approach to data analyses and understanding. Whilst central government has always emphasised the devolved nature of the programme, in practice, Pathfinders had to deal with a degree of constraint in the analysis and interpretation of the problem and in the delivery of solutions.

However, the environment in which locally derived data can be used (e.g., local council tax registers) has changed, with a risk averse environment predominating, and public service agreements creating obstacles to shared intelligence and data. Privatisation practices and the trend towards public service partnerships in which local authorities contract out the delivery of IT and 'data rich' services such as the administration of housing benefit, will undermine their ability to use data for purposes other than those specified in the partnership agreement. Privatisation of data handling services and contracting out practices, such as Birmingham City Council's 10 year preferred strategic partnering arrangement with Capita (providing IT and business services), make it more difficult for local authorities and local strategic partnerships to develop *ad hoc* monitoring systems, where business partnerships and joint ventures of this nature are in existence.

Public service partnerships of this type offer unique opportunities to develop monitoring systems that can capture neighbourhood changes by bringing together a wealth of data at individual and neighbourhood level that can be used to explain changes and inform policy responses. However, the terms of reference for such public service partnerships tend to be based on a lowest common denominator with the partnership emphasising investment in hardware and software to integrate systems for efficiency and e-governance objectives. This fails to take advantage of the underlying data for wider strategic goals (such as planning and regeneration). The danger is that many local authorities may cede control of their data, so that it is more expensive in future to interrogate for purposes beyond that of the immediate end service user requirements. This will result in higher revenue costs to service *ad hoc* demands placed on IT systems. There will inevitably be significant contractual costs attached to the local authority re-using and analysing its own data, unless this was considered in the system's planning and implementation at contract stage. These concerns about privatisation also raise concern that local authorities need to explore the full 'spatial dimensions' of IT services and public service contracts before proceeding to long-term binding agreements. This will reduce costs and protect the interests of consumers and council tax payers by using readily available administrative data and in-house systems to monitor changes in the housing market. The majority of the Pathfinders tended to fall back on official population estimates and projections based on the census. While there was some evidence of innovation, where Pathfinders used local administrative data sets to track population change, arguably more could be done to develop local housing market monitoring systems that are more dynamic and less reliant on periodic censuses. This is especially important within the context of a 'plan, monitor and manage' planning regime, of which we say more in the next section. One available option for local authorities and multi-area agreement authorities is to consider the use of Primary Care Trust GP records (the Exeter System) to monitor population change at the small area level. Whilst this has disadvantages (e.g., failure for some groups such as men aged 18-30 to register and problems with change of address where patients fail to register with their local GP), it does have its advantages in providing a basis on which population trends and vulnerable groups (e.g., under 5s), with particular housing needs, can be monitored or assessed for their impact on future population trends and housing demand.

Planning and regional housing markets

The Planning and Compulsory Purchase Act 2004 introduced new statutory planning documents in the form of Local Development Frameworks (LDFs) and regional spatial strategies (RSSs). In planning for housing provision, these effectively formalised a shift in approach away from the former 'predict and provide' methodology to that of 'plan, monitor and manage' (PMM). The PMM process, if properly conducted, introduces a set of mechanisms that are highly appropriate for dealing with low and changing demand for housing, as compared to a 'predict and provide' approach (which can take some of the share of responsibility for contributing to the underlying problems of over-supply that contributed to low demand). However, a PMM approach requires that the relationship between Pathfinders' plans (especially their masterplanning work), and the new planning hierarchy from RSS down to LDFs, needs to be consistent. Because of the realisation that a well-functioning housing market might 'unlock' economic growth, this issue has become critically important and was central to the competitiveness 'strand' of HMR. Together, these changes to the planning system, as well as Kate Barker's recommendations and guidance within Planning Policy Statement 3 (PPS3, Planning for Housing), have significant implications for housing renewal. They promote a language of economic and housing growth that was previously considered to be an issue only for the South of England.

The ability to dynamically monitor demand and adjust the future release of sites for new housing is crucial in this respect, but Pathfinders have found themselves at the interface of competing local and regional aspirations. Pathfinders must reconcile housing requirements for multiple local authorities in their areas, while influencing planning policy across those, and other adjacent, authorities in their entirety. The main dangers arise when local authorities harbour 'growth' aspirations at the same time as trying to manage low demand. There is an immense risk that they could fall back into the old trap of viewing local housing market weakness as being simply a neighbourhood issue. While overall 'targets' for housing provision contained within RSS could be accommodated, experience of low and changing demand would suggest that local qualitative and spatial expressions of these targets are of equal importance. Closer integration of Regional Housing Strategies and Integrated Regional Strategies (IRS) will help, as well as the further development of Strategic

Housing Market Assessments (SHMAS, see below), but the onus is clearly on monitoring, the acknowledgment of the sub-regional scale of the relationship between supply and demand, and awareness of the impact of developments in adjacent regions.

The Northern Way was considered to be a response to these issues. It highlighted a £29 billion gap annually between the northern regions' productivity and the UK average and set out a strategy for closing this gap. It was based on the integration of social, economic and environmental objectives and, importantly, inter-regional working; the promotion of connectivity between and within markets, and a focus on the city regions as the main delivery agents to promote sustainability (Northern Way Steering Group, 2004).

Growth aspirations, such as those in the Northern Way, encouraged the upward shift of regional housing targets through the adoption of more bullish economic scenarios. Local authorities began to convince themselves of their ability to absorb market restructuring *and* the significant release of new housing sites. But, the success of the former is potentially contingent on the restriction of the latter.

We have argued throughout that this environment has resulted in Pathfinders placing a greater strategic emphasis on demonstrating how housing renewal will bring about economic growth. In some cases, this was being translated as housing growth, i.e., the net addition of dwelling stock over and above that projected for reasons of natural population change. Reasons why this may be the case vary. In some instances, additional housing was always part of the plan. In some cases, it is not unreasonable to expect that the house price growth and worsening affordability (even in 'low-demand' areas) during the period 2003-2007 blinded Pathfinders (and government) into thinking that there is no longer a surplus of housing stock. The most worrying scenario, however, is where problems with implementation, strategic alignment, or partnership working have led to a fallback position of going for growth – hence avoiding the difficult and politically divisive issue of restructuring. In particular, there has been much concern that Pathfinder teams and their delivery partners lack the necessary skills and capacity to put some of the more radical HMR plans into operation. This, along with concerns about the length of time it takes to put these plans into action, was one of the main findings of a select committee enquiry into the low-demand Pathfinders (HC 295-I, 2004-05).

A concern with new housing supply leads us back to the 'question of scale', which we suggest is of great importance in the future direction and evaluation of market renewal policy. In adopting a growth strategy, one that eschews a re-balancing of supply in favour of promoting new housing release, there is a real risk of revisiting old mistakes. First, is the untrammelled supply of new housing on edge-city sites, or, of continued new RSL general needs rental provision at a time even when demand was weakening: '...*who dared say...that there were really too many houses in their area?'* (Keenan *et al.*, 1999, p.711). This is an historic legacy known to have directly contributed to market weakness. The second point is that HMR could be, *'...''normalised'' into just another kind of physical regeneration programme'* (Cole and Nevin, 2004, p.70), one that focuses on neighbourhood level problems without tackling underlying structural inequalities.

A *changing demand* as opposed to *low demand* response, recognises that local economies continually change and that the housing market response lags, but needs to be understood. But, equally the response must challenge itself by trying to influence economic policy. The days of industrial policy are long gone and a strategic response that is synergistic with local economic policy is now what is expected.

The debate on changing and low demand was however lost, so that the HMR policy was truncated to a policy that was designed to tackle the worst manifestations of low demand, but to do this in a way that would alter the pattern of demand so that house prices would be stabilised and neighbourhoods would be turned around. Whilst the worst manifestations of low demand have been largely eradicated in the Pathfinder areas, the changing nature of demand will mean that problems of demand and supply will never be fully eradicated. Demand for housing will always be subject to change and the asymmetry between housing and labour markets will mean that there are constant adjustments and shifts in demand for areas and types of housing. HMR has been used to illustrate both intelligence and intervention in the housing market as a mechanism to address asymmetry. But, how can housing markets be kept in step with the economy?

At times, the evidence base and prospectuses for HMR reflected a world of limited horizons based on regional economies running limitless credit and purchasing power (see, for example, Figure 6.1). This is not a failure of the Pathfinders or their efforts;

Figure 6.1: Shopping and football – a depiction of the future economy within a 2005/06 Housing Market Renewal annual report

Source: NewHeartlands (2006, p.19).

it is a collective failure of economic and housing market logics to offer more sustainable alternatives. The failure of imagination is therefore a collective failure of government and governance. Whether the credit crunch has forced all of us to think more critically and to challenge some of our underlying assumptions is yet to be seen.

There does need to be a re-evaluation of the basis of the local and regional economy and what kind of housing and neighbourhoods that can be supported. The success of Housing Market Renewal is premised on the success of the existing economic model that underpins regeneration and economic development of towns and cities, but the credit crunch has demonstrated the fragility of this. Building in resilience to our housing and labour markets will be the biggest challenge in the future. Nowhere in the evidence base for HMR was there a consideration of alternative economic scenarios, or economic outcomes that may have promoted wider caution and behaviour in the broader housing market, and considered the potential of such a significant scaling down of the national and regional economy signalled by the credit crunch. Future evidence building will need to be more robust in its appraisal of risk and the resilience of the market.

Looked at through a different lens, HMR has been responsible for moving the agenda forward considerably. Strategic Housing Market Assessments (SHMAs) were introduced largely on the back of the HMR development of evidence and 'drivers of change' and have their roots in the Sustainable Communities Plan. They are designed to help local authorities and partnerships understand the housing market and plan accordingly. However, SHMAs are a data driven and 'tick-box' approach to understanding the market, which need to be supplemented by guidance and best practice on the interpretation of data and on the softer 'process' driven elements. Best practice needs to be developed, not least in the commissioning and interpretation of evidence by consultants. In some cases, the consultant may have a vested interest in the commissioning of new housing and regeneration. Therefore, there should be a separation of these activities and scrutiny of declared interests.

Switching to a more sustainable pattern of growth will necessitate several changes. The underlying drivers of the market will remain the asymmetry of housing and labour markets. In the new market conditions, the carbon-based urban form (housing, economy, urban forms and styles of residential developments) of the core cities and older conurbations will appear anachronistic. The urban form of the future may have to consider more polycentric forms with the conurbations needing to diversify as well as intensify their land-use patterns. This will mean re-designing our built-up areas so that they can accommodate more urban farming and recreation space to enable a more sustainable pattern of production and consumption. This challenges the conventional narrative of the 'knowledge' and 'creative' economy. Different kinds of knowledge need to be emphasised and some old ones will need to be revisited. Diversifying the housing and neighbourhoods within the core cities and other older conurbations will enhance their contribution to environmental sustainability. Higher quality, more ecologically friendly housing will offer direct benefits. But, arguably the greatest contribution will be indirect, coming from reducing the need to travel for work and food shopping as households can once again choose to live closer to where they need to be.

Beyond this, the interpretation and preparation of intelligence supporting SHMAs should be triangulated and tested using foresight and scenario testing techniques and there is a need to develop more interactive models of housing demand, including how evidence maps onto local neighbourhoods. Similarly, we need to understand the underlying composition of economic growth and its implication for neighbourhood and housing preferences. SHMAS (and HMR plans in a 'growth context') are very supply driven. Increasingly, the tools of the housing planning system (such as PPS 3, identifying forward supplies of land and their viability, and assessing market demand in SHMAs), have to be alive to the possibilities of managing demand and not just be about delivering supply. We must not forget that part of the low-demand problem was caused by 'structural' changes to the supply over periods of time: decentralisation; suburbanisation; and a surfeit of new, cheap 'boxes' in places that did not really need them. The same could easily happen again. Not that much has changed in ten years!

Governing places

Taking this forward will require a refreshing of our organisational and leadership requirements. The backlash to HMR was in part a defence of the vernacular housing form (the *terrace* house or the *suburban* ex-council semi), and the expression of a tangible set of objections in the face of an abstracted set of strategic considerations. This highlights the need to develop new approaches and ways of thinking that are not tainted by political dogma and are open to effective dialogue and debate. This extends into reconciling political tensions that vie for ownership of solutions across spatial scales and that lead to gaps in the democratic representation of space and accountability. The Housing Market Renewal story spans thinking from the spatially bounded 'worst estates' to a competitiveness approach that is susceptible to an erosion of local political accountability. But, the rescaling of housing issues and the inter-connections between housing markets and neighbourhoods means that we have to think beyond the estate; beyond the street. The concept of *leadership of place* (Trickett and Lee, 2010, forthcoming), emphasises a more nuanced style, incorporating a broader spatial literacy and a whole systems approach, which aims to tackle the symptoms and the causes of dysfunctional housing market performance. HMR more neatly falls into the territory of 'place leadership' incorporating a shared thematic and spatial understanding of the market and how to intervene.

During the past decade the 'place shaping' and 'place making' agendas, and the roles of local authorities and other stakeholders in creating places that people want to live has grown in importance and will continue to do so. Place is seen as important within a competitive global economy with cities seen as the focal point for competitiveness and creativity:

> *...along with an increased concern for cities generally, there is a growing recognition that the centres of those cities are an increasingly important economic asset...the key drivers of a modern economy are innovation and skills, economic and cultural diversity, connectivity, strategic decision-making capacity and place quality. In particular place quality is an important element of the* [location] *factors which are crucial to attract investors, employers and skilled workers to cities* (Parkinson, 2007, p.4).

HMR was, alongside the city region debate and the changing governance and planning infrastructure within England (cf. the development of regional spatial strategies, the sub-national review of economic development and regeneration, the Barker Review of Planning and Housing and the introduction of Strategic Housing Market Assessments), a necessary precursor to the language of 'place shaping', Comprehensive Area Assessments and the 'leadership of place'. Whilst HMR is a significant departure from estate-based interventions and intelligence typified by the 'worst estates' of the late 1990s, the journey has not ended. Where, therefore, do we expect the HMR story to end or lead? In the next period of housing policy for the UK, the city centre market will require a new wave of creative strategic commissioning to re-balance the market and to respond to the needs of both local communities and the underlying 'real economy' (LGA, 2008). Whilst we have argued that the social exclusion agenda was supplanted by a competitiveness agenda, and that Housing Market Renewal was one of the most significant and emblematic policies reflecting that repositioning of New Labour narrative, this may of course be a false dichotomy. Is the social exclusion agenda sacrificed as a result of a competitiveness agenda? What price the neglect of low-demand areas without intervention? The answer, of course, is that a policy that promotes both competitiveness and safeguards inclusion can be compatible. The answer will continue to be one of detail in the implementation and the degree of incision into the housing market needed in order to balance these two competing ends.

References

Allen, C. (2008) *Housing Market Renewal and Social Class*, London: Routledge.

Allen, J. and Hamnett, C. (1991) *Housing and Labour Markets: Building the Connections*, Oxford: Routledge.

Amin, A. (Ed) (1994) *Post-Fordism: a Reader*, Oxford: Blackwell.

Andersson, R. and Bråmå, Å. (2004) Selective migration in Swedish distressed neighbourhoods: can area-based urban policies counteract segregation processes?, *Housing Studies*, 19 (4), pp.517-539.

Ashley, J. (2001) John Prescott: sinking fast, *New Statesman*, 7 May 2001.

Audit Commission (2005) *Housing Market Renewal: best practice handbook*, London: Audit Commission.

Audit Commission (2006) *Housing Market Renewal Annual Review 2005/06*, London: Audit Commission.

Audit Commission (2009) Use of GIS and Sustainability Modelling tool for local housing markets – Birmingham City Council, *Good Practice Case Studies* [website], available from: http://www.audit-commission.gov.uk/housing/goodpractice/ Strategicapproachtohousing [accessed 5 December 2009].

Bains, J. (2006) *Futures Housing 2020: Housing Needs, Choices and Aspirations of South Asian Communities in the West Midlands*, Birmingham: Ashram Housing Association.

Barker, K. (2004) *Delivering Stability: Securing our Future Housing Needs*, London: HM Treasury.

Barker, K. (2006) *Barker Review of Land Use Planning*, final report, London: HM Treasury.

BCC (Birmingham City Council) (2005) *Birmingham City Council Housing Strategy*, Birmingham: Birmingham City Council.

Blair, T. (1997) The Will to Win (speech delivered at the Aylesbury Estate, London, 2 June 1997), available from: http://archive.cabinetoffice.gov.uk/seu/newsa52f. html?id=400 [accessed 10 August 2007].

Boddy, M. and Parkinson, M. (2004) *City Matters: Competitiveness, Cohesion and Urban Governance*, Bristol: Policy Press.

Bramley, G., Pawson, H., Hague, C., McIntosh, S. and Third, H. (2000) *Low Demand Housing and Unpopular Neighbourhoods*, London: Department for the Environment, Transport and the Regions (DETR).

Bridging NewcastleGateshead (2003) *Creating Places Where More People Want to Live* (Housing Market Renewal prospectus), Newcastle upon Tyne: Bridging NewcastleGateshead.

Burfitt, A. and Ferrari, E. (2008) The housing and neighbourhood impacts of knowledge-based economic development following industrial closure, *Policy Studies*, 29 (3), pp.293-304.

Burrows, R. (1999) Residential mobility and residualisation in social housing in England, *Journal of Social Policy*, 28 (1), pp.27-52.

Burrows, R. and Rhodes, D. (1998) *Unpopular Places? Area Disadvantage and the Geography of Misery in England*, Bristol: Policy Press.

Cameron, S. (2006) From low demand to rising aspirations: Housing Market Renewal within regional and neighbourhood regeneration policy, *Housing Studies*, 21 (1), pp.3-16.

Cameron, S. and Field, A. (2000) Community, ethnicity and neighbourhood, *Housing Studies*, 15 (6), pp.827-843.

Clapham, D. (2002) Housing pathways: a post modern analytical framework, *Housing, Theory and Society*, 19, pp.57-68.

CLG (Communities and Local Government) (2006a) *Planning Policy Statement 3: Housing*, London: Communities and Local Government.

CLG (2006b) *Housing Market Renewal Pathfinders – Respect Protocol*, London: Communities and Local Government.

CLG (2007a) *Homes for the Future: more affordable, more sustainable*, Cm 7191, London: The Stationery Office.

CLG (2007b) *Strategic Housing Market Assessments: Practice Guidance*, London: Communities and Local Government, available from: http://www.communities. gov.uk/documents/planningandbuilding/pdf/323201.pdf [accessed 1 July 2009].

CML (Council for Mortgage Lenders) (2007) *Buy-to-Let Market Summary*, London: Council for Mortgage Lenders, available from: http://www.cml.org.uk/cml/statistics [accessed 6 September 2007].

Cole, I. and Ferrari, E. (2007) Connectivity of place and housing market change: the case of Birmingham, pp.57-80 in: Flint, J. and Robinson, D. (Eds) *Community Cohesion in Crisis? New Dimensions of Diversity and Difference*, Bristol: Policy Press.

Cole, I. and Flint, J. (2007) *Housing Affordability, Clearance and Relocation in the Housing Market Renewal Pathfinders*, Coventry: Chartered Institute of Housing.

Cole, I., Kane, S. and Robinson, D. (1999) *Changing Demand, Changing Neighbourhoods: the Response of Social Landlords*, Sheffield: Centre for Regional Economic and Social Research, Sheffield Hallam University.

Cole, I. and Nevin, B. (2004) *The Road to Renewal: The Early Development of the Housing Market Renewal Programme in England*, York: Joseph Rowntree Foundation.

Collinge, C. (1999) Self-organization of society by scale: a spatial reworking of regulation theory, *Environment and Planning D: Society and Space*, 17, pp.554-74.

Corporate Watch (2009) Pathfinder profiteers, *Corporate Watch Newsletter*, 30 September 2009, available from: www.corporatewatch.org/?lid=2574 [accessed 19 February 2010].

Counsell, D. and Haughton, G. (2003) Regional planning tensions: planning for economic growth and sustainable development in two contrasting English regions, *Environment and Planning C: Government and Policy*, 21, pp.225-239.

Crook, A. D. H., Monk, S., Rowley, S. and Whitehead, C. M. E. (2006) Planning gain and the supply of new affordable housing in England: understanding the numbers, *Town Planning Review*, 77 (3), pp.353-73.

Cullingworth, J. B. and Nadin, V. (1994) *Town and Country Planning in Britain*, 11th edition, London: Routledge.

CURS (Centre for Urban and Regional Studies) (2004) *Northern Way Housing Study*, Newcastle upon Tyne: The Northern Way.

Davies, J. S. (2001) *Partnerships and regimes: the politics of urban regeneration in the UK*, Aldershot: Ashgate.

DETR (Department of the Environment, Transport and the Regions) (2000a) *Responding to Low Demand Housing and Unpopular Neighbourhoods: a Guide to Good Practice*, London: Department of the Environment, Transport and the Regions.

DETR (2000b) *Quality and Choice: A Decent Home for All – the Housing Green Paper*, London: Department for the Environment, Transport and the Regions.

DHW (Department of Housing and Works) (2001) *Housing Strategy WA: Drivers of Change – Influences on Housing*, East Perth, Australia: Government of Western Australia.

DoE (Department of the Environment) (1995) *Our Future Homes: Opportunities, Choices and Responsibilities: The Government's Housing Policies for England and Wales*, CM 2901, London: Her Majesty's Stationery Office.

DTZ (2007) *Sheffield City Centre Housing Market Study* (Executive Summary), Sheffield: Sheffield City Council, available from: www.sheffield.gov.uk/index.asp?pgid=113180&mtype=print [accessed 4 September 2007].

Egan Review (2004) *The Egan Review: Skills for Sustainable Communities*, London: Office of the Deputy Prime Minister and Royal Institute of British Architects.

Ferrari, E. (2007) Housing Market Renewal in an era of new housing supply, *People, Place and Policy Online*, 1 (3), pp.124-135.

Fitzpatrick, S. (2005) *Poverty and Place*, Centre for Housing Policy working paper, York: Centre for Housing Policy, University of York and Joseph Rowntree Foundation.

Forrest, R. and Murie, A. (1983) Residualisation and council housing: aspects of the changing social relations of tenure, *Journal of Social Policy*, 12 (4), pp.453-68.

Forrest, R., Murie, A. and Williams, P. (1990) *Home Ownership: Differentiation and Fragmentation*, London: Unwin Hyman.

Galster, G. (1996) William Grigsby and the analysis of housing sub-markets and filtering, *Urban Studies*, 33 (10), pp.1797-1805.

Galster, G. (1997) Comparing demand-side and supply-side housing policies: sub-market and spatial perspectives, *Housing Studies*, 33 (10), pp.561-577.

Galster, G. (2001) On the nature of neighbourhood, *Urban Studies*, 38 (12), pp.2111-2124.

Gibney, J., Copeland, S. and Murie, A. (2009) Toward a 'new' strategic leadership of place for the knowledge-based economy, *Leadership*, 5 (1), pp.5-23.

Goodchild, B. and Hickman, P. (2004) *Towards a Regional Strategy for the North of England? An Assessment of the Northern Way and its Growth Vision*, unpublished seminar paper, Sheffield: Centre for Regional Economic and Social Research, Sheffield Hallam University.

Goodchild, B. and Hickman, P. (2006) Towards a regional strategy for the North of England? An assessment of 'The Northern Way', *Regional Studies*, 40 (1), pp.121-133.

Great Britain (2002) *The Government's Response to the Transport, Local Government and the Regions Select Committee's Sixth Report on Empty Homes*, Cm 5514, London: The Stationery Office.

Groves, R., Lee, P., Murie, A. and Nevin, B. (2001) *Private Rented Housing in Liverpool: an Overview of Current Market Conditions*, Research Report No. 3, Liverpool: Liverpool City Council.

Groves, R. and Murie, A. (2001) *Private Rented Housing in Liverpool*, Liverpool: Liverpool City Council.

Hall S. and Hickman P. (2004). Bulldozing the North and concreting over the South? The United Kingdom government's Sustainable Communities Plan, *Géocarrefour*, 79 (2), pp.143-152.

Harding, A., Deas, I., Evans, R. and Wilks-Heeg, S. (2004) Reinventing cities in a restructuring region? The rhetoric and reality of renaissance in Liverpool and Manchester, pp.33-50 in: Boddy, M. and Parkinson, M. (Eds) *City Matters: Competitiveness, Cohesion and Urban Governance*, Bristol: Policy Press.

HBF (House Builders' Federation) (undated) *North East House Builders Demand Plan for Growth Not Decline*, news release available from: http://www.hbf.co.uk/news/news.asp?id=99pr12 [accessed 18 October 1999]

HC 240-I (2001-02) *Empty Homes*, sixth report of the House of Commons Transport, Local Government and the Regions committee, session 2001-02, London: The Stationery Office.

HC 295-I (2004-05) *Empty Homes and Low Demand Pathfinders*, eighth report of the House of Commons, ODPM: Housing, Planning, Local Government and the Regions committee, session 2004-05, London: The Stationery Office.

HC 977-II (2005-06) *Is There a Future for Regional Government?*, written evidence, Office of the Deputy Prime Minister: Housing, Planning, Local Government and the Regions committee, session 2005-06, London: The Stationery Office.

Hills, J. (2007) *Ends and means: the future roles of social housing in England*, London: Centre for Analysis of Social Exclusion, London School of Economics.

HM Treasury (2007) *PSA Delivery Agreement 20: Increase Long Term Housing Supply and Affordability*, October 2007, London: Her Majesty's Stationery Office, available at: http://www.hm-treasury.gov.uk/d/pbr_csr07_psa20.pdf [accessed 10 August 2009].

Holmans, A. (2001) *Housing Demand and Need in England 1996-2016*, London: TCPA and NHF.

Holmans, A. E. and Simpson, M. (1999) *Low Demand: Separating Fact from Fiction*, Coventry: Chartered Institute of Housing.

House of Commons (2008) *Housing Market Renewal: Pathfinders*, thirty-fifth report of the Committee of Public Accounts, session 2007-08, London: The Stationery Office.

Housing Corporation (2006) *Neighbourhoods and Communities Strategy*, October 2006, London: Housing Corporation.

HUD (Department of Housing and Urban Development) (2000) *State of the Cities Data Systems (SOCDS)*, electronic data source, Washington, DC: Department of Housing and Urban Development, available from: http://socds.huduser.org/socds_home.html [accessed 5 November 2007].

Imrie, R. and Raco, M. (2003) Community and the changing nature of urban policy, pp.3-36 in: Imrie, R. and Raco, M. (Eds) *Urban Renaissance? New Labour, Community and Urban Policy*, Bristol: Policy Press.

Jones, C., Leishman, C. and Watkins, C. (2004) Intra-urban migration and housing submarkets: theory and evidence, *Housing Studies*, 19 (2), pp.269-283.

Jones, C. and Murie, A. (2006) *The Right to Buy*, Oxford: Blackwell.

Jones, C. and Watkins, C. (2009) *Housing Markets and Public Policy*, Chichester: Wiley.

Jones, P. and Evans, J. (2006) Urban regeneration, governance and the state: exploring notions of distance and proximity, *Urban Studies*, 43 (9), pp.1491-1509.

Kay, A. (2005) A Critique of the Use of Path Dependency in Policy Studies, *Public Administration*, 83 (3), pp.553-571.

Keenan, P. (1998) Residential mobility and demand: a case history from Newcastle, in Lowe, S., Spencer, S. and Keenan, P. (Eds) *Housing Abandonment in Britain: Studies in the Causes and Effects of Low Demand Housing*, York: Centre for Housing Policy, University of York.

Keenan P., Lowe. S. and Spencer. S. (1999) Housing abandonment in inner cities – the politics of low demand for housing, *Housing Studies*, 14 (5), pp.703-716.

Kemp, P. (1998) *Housing Benefit: Time for Reform*, York: Joseph Rowntree Foundation.

Kirchner, P. (2000) The German-owned manufacturing sector in the North-East of England, *European Planning Studies*, 8 (5), pp.601-617.

Leather, P., Cole, I. and Ferrari, E. with Flint, J., Robinson, D., Simpson, C., Hopley, M. (2007) *National Evaluation of the HMR Pathfinder Programme: Baseline Report*, London: Communities and Local Government.

Leather, P., Lee, P. and Ferrari, E. (2003) *Changing Housing Markets in Cheshire, Cumbria and Lancashire*, Birmingham: Centre for Urban and Regional Studies, University of Birmingham.

Leather, P., Lee, P. and Murie, A. (2002) *North East England: Changing Housing Markets and Urban Regeneration*, Birmingham: Centre for Urban and Regional Studies, University of Birmingham.

Lee, P. and Ferrari, E. (2005) *Housing Demand in Coventry: Preferences and Aspirations*, Stage 2 Summary Report, Coventry: Coventry Group of Housing Associations.

Lee, P. and Ferrari, E. (2007) *Changes in Deprivation 1981-2001*, CURS working paper, Birmingham: Centre for Urban and Regional Studies, University of Birmingham.

Lee, P., Hall, S., Barber, A. and Leather, P. (2002) *Neighbourhood Trajectories and Social Exclusion in Wakefield*, Birmingham: Centre for Urban and Regional Studies, University of Birmingham.

Lee, P., Leather, P. and Ferrari, E. (2003) *Birmingham and Solihull Eastern Corridor Study*, final report, Birmingham: Centre for Urban and Regional Studies, University of Birmingham.

Lee, P., Leather, P., Goodson, L., Phillimore, J. and Murie, A. (2002) *Developing a Sub-Regional Investment Strategy for North Staffordshire*, Birmingham: Centre for Urban and Regional Studies, University of Birmingham.

Lee, P., Leather, P., Murie, A., Phillimore, J. and Goodson, L. (2002) *Yorkshire and Humberside: Changing Housing Markets and Urban Regeneration*, Birmingham: Centre for Urban and Regional Studies, University of Birmingham.

Lee, P. and Murie, A. (1997) *Poverty, Housing Tenure and Social Exclusion*, Bristol: Policy Press.

Lee, P. and Murie, A. (2002) The poor city: national and local perspectives on changes in residential patterns in the British city, pp.59-87 in: Marcuse, P. and van Kempen, R. (Eds) *Of States and Cities: a Partitioning of Urban Space*, Oxford: Oxford University Press.

Lee, P. and Murie, A. (2004) The role of housing in delivering a knowledge economy, *Built Environment*, 30 (3), pp.235-245.

Lee, P., Murie, A. and Gordon, D. (1995) *Area Measures of Deprivation: a Study of Current Methods and Best Practices in the Identification of Poor Areas in Great Britain*, Birmingham: Centre for Urban and Regional Studies, University of Birmingham.

Lee, P. and Nevin, B. (2002) *Renewing the Housing Market of Liverpool's Inner Core*, Research Report No. 8, Liverpool: Liverpool City Council.

Lee, P. and Nevin, B. (2003) Changing demand for housing: restructuring markets and the public policy framework, *Housing Studies*, 18 (1), pp.65-86.

Leunig, T. and Swaffield, J. (2007) *Cities Unlimited: Making Urban Regeneration Work*, London: Policy Exchange.

Levitas, R. (1998) *The Inclusive Society: Social Exclusion and New Labour*, Basingstoke: Macmillan.

Lewis, O. (1966) *La Vida: A Puerto Rican Family in the Culture of Poverty – San Juan and New York*, New York: Random House.

LGA (Local Government Association) (2008) *Councils and the Housing Crisis*, London: Local Government Association.

Long, D. (1999) *Social Housing and RDAs: a Common Agenda*, Liverpool: European Institute for Urban Affairs, Liverpool John Moores University.

Long, D. and Hutchins, M. (2003) *A Toolkit of Indicators of Sustainable Communities* (3rd edition), London: Housing Corporation and European Institute of Urban Affairs.

Lowe, S., Spencer, S. and Keenan, P. (Eds) (1998) *Housing Abandonment in Britain: Studies in the Causes and Effects of Low Demand Housing*, York: Centre for Housing Policy, University of York.

Lyons, M. (2007) *Place-shaping: a Shared Ambition for the Future of Local Government*, final report of the Lyons Inquiry into Local Government, London: The Stationery Office.

Mandelson, P. (1997) *Labour's Next Steps: Tackling Social Exclusion*, London: Fabian Society.

MRUK (2004) *Transform South Yorkshire Housing Aspirations Survey*, draft final report, December 2004, Sheffield: Transform South Yorkshire, available from: http://www.transformsouthyorkshire.org.uk/documents/Final_Report_Insider_Percepti ons_Study.doc [accessed 19 January 2010].

Mullins, D. (1998) Rhetoric and reality in housing policy, pp.246-259 in: Marsh, A. and Mullins, D. (Eds) *Housing and Public Policy: Citizenship, Choice and Control*, Buckingham: Open University Press.

Murie A., Nevin, B., and Leather P. (1998) *Changing Demand and Unpopular Housing*, working paper 4, London: Housing Corporation.

Murray, C. (1990) *The Emerging British Underclass*, London: Institute of Economic Affairs.

Musterd, S. (2006) Segregation, urban space and the resurgent city, *Urban Studies*, 43 (8), pp.1325-1340.

NAO (National Audit Office) (2007) *Department for Communities and Local Government: Housing Market Renewal*, report by the comptroller and auditor general, London: The Stationery Office.

NHPAU (National Housing and Planning Advice Unit) (2007) *Affordability Matters*, Tichfield, Hampshire: National Housing and Planning Advice Unit, available from: http://www.communities.gov.uk/publications/housing/affordabilitymatters [accessed 4 September 2007].

Nevin, B. (2001) *Housing Market Renewal: Submission to the Comprehensive Spending Review*, London: National Housing Federation.

Nevin, B., Goodson, L., Lee, P. and Phillimore, J. (2001) *Housing Market Change and Urban Regeneration: Achieving Sustainable Neighbourhoods in North West Birmingham*, Birmingham: Birmingham City Council and Advantage West Midlands.

Nevin, B., Hall, S. and Srbjlanin, A. (2000) *Stabilising the Population of Liverpool: Employment Markets and Housing Choice*, Liverpool: Liverpool City Council.

Nevin B. and Lee P. (2003) *Understanding the Liverpool Housing Market: Reversing Decline and Managing Change*, Research Report No. 9, Liverpool: Liverpool City Council.

Nevin, B., Lee, P., Goodson, L., Murie, A. and Phillimore, J. (2000) *Changing Housing Markets and Urban Regeneration in the M62 Corridor*, Birmingham: Centre for Urban and Regional Studies, University of Birmingham.

Nevin B., Lee P., Murie A., Goodson L. and Phillimore J. (2001) *The West Midlands Housing Markets: Changing Demand, Decentralisation and Urban Regeneration*, Birmingham: Centre for Urban and Regional Studies, University of Birmingham.

Nevin, B., Lee, P. and Phillimore, J. (1999) *Measuring the Sustainability of Neighbourhoods in Liverpool*, Liverpool: Liverpool City Council.

NewHeartlands (2006) *Annual Report 2005-2006*, Liverpool: NewHeartlands, available from: http://newheartlands.co.uk/assets/_files/documents/jun_07/nh__1183110467_NH_ANN_REP_06_LINKED.pdf [accessed 16 March 2010].

Northern Way Steering Group (2004) *Making it Happen: the Northern Way*, Newcastle upon Tyne: Northern Way Steering Group.

ODPM (Office of the Deputy Prime Minister) (2003) *Sustainable Communities: Building for the Future*, London: Office of the Deputy Prime Minister.

ODPM (2004a) *Competitive European Cities: Where Do the Core Cities Stand?*, London: Office of the Deputy Prime Minister.

ODPM (2004b) *Housing Market Assessments*, London: Office of the Deputy Prime Minister.

ODPM (2004c) *PSA Target 6 – Planning Performance*, London, Office of the Deputy Prime Minister, available from: http://www.communities.gov.uk/documents/corporate/pdf/psa-target6.pdf [accessed 10 August 2009].

ODPM (2005a) *Sustainable Communities: Homes for All*, Cm 6424, London: Office of the Deputy Prime Minister.

ODPM (2005b) *Market Renewal Pathfinders: Invitation to Submit a Scheme Update and Independent Scrutiny Framework* (February 2005), London: Office of the Deputy Prime Minister.

ODPM (2005c) *Delivering Sustainable Development* (Planning Policy Statement 1), London: Office of the Deputy Prime Minister.

ODPM (2006) *A Framework for City Regions*, London: Office of the Deputy Prime Minister.

Our City Region (2005) *Memorandum by Our City Region Partnership*, written evidence RG31, pp.Ev71-Ev75 in: HC 977-II (2005-06).

Parkinson, M. (2007) *The Birmingham City Centre Masterplan: The Visioning Study*, Liverpool: European Institute for Urban Affairs, Liverpool John Moores University.

Pattison, G. (2004) Planning for decline: the 'D'-village policy of County Durham, UK, *Planning Perspectives*, 19 (3), pp.311-332.

Pawson H. and Bramley G. (2000) Understanding recent trends in residential mobility in council housing in England, *Urban Studies*, 37 (8), pp.1231-1259.

Pawson, H., Jones, C., Donohoe, T., Netto, G., Fancy, C., Clegg, S. and Thomas, A. (2006) *Monitoring the Longer Term Impact of Choice Based Lettings*, London: Communities and Local Government.

PiA (Partners in Action) (2003) *Transformation and Cohesion*, Housing Market Renewal prospectus, Oldham: Partners in Action.

Pike, A., Champion, T., Coombes, M., Humphrey, L. and Tomaney, J. (2006) *The Economic Viability and Self-Containment of Geographical Economies: A Framework for Analysis*, London: Office of the Deputy Prime Minister, available from: http://www.communities.gov.uk/documents/corporate/pdf/144515 [accessed 5 September 2007].

Popkin, S. J., Katz, B., Cunningham, M. K., Brown, K. D., Gustafson, J. and Turner, M. A. (2004) *A Decade of HOPE IV: research findings and policy challenges*, Washington DC: Urban Institute.

Power, A. and Mumford, K. (1999) *The Slow Death of Great Cities? Urban Abandonment or Urban Renaissance*, York: Joseph Rowntree Foundation.

RNS (Renew North Staffordshire) (2004) *Market Renewal Prospectus*, March 2004, Stoke on Trent: Renew North Staffordshire.

Robinson, D. (2003) Housing governance in the English regions: emerging structures, limits and potentials, *Housing Studies*, 18 (2), pp.249-267.

Robinson, D., Ferrari, E. and Cowerd, S. (2005) *Housing Market Intelligence in the HMR Pathfinders*, Sheffield: Sheffield Hallam University Centre for Regional Economic and Social Research.

Robson, B. (1988) *Those Inner Cities: Reconciling the Economic and Social Aims of Urban Policy*, Oxford: Clarendon Press.

Robson, B. (2003) Sustainable communities: more action plan than strategy, *Town and Country Planning*, 27 (3), p.98.

Room, G. (1995) *Beyond the Threshold: the Measurement and Analysis of Social Exclusion*, Bristol: Policy Press.

RTPI (Royal Town Planning Institute) and CLG (Communities and Local Government) (2008) *Measuring the Outcomes of Spatial Planning in England*, London: Royal Town Planning Institute.

Save Britain's Heritage (2006) *Pathfinder*, London: Save Britain's Heritage.

Saunders, P. (1990) *A Nation of Home Owners*, London: Unwin Hyman.

Sefton, T. (forthcoming) *Using the British Household Panel Study to explore changes in housing tenure in England*, CASEpaper, London: Centre for Analysis of Social Exclusion, London School of Economics.

SEU (Social Exclusion Unit) (1998) Speech given by the prime minister on Monday 8 December 1997, at the Stockwell Park School, Lambeth, at the launch of the Government's Social Exclusion Unit.

SEU (2000) *Unpopular Housing: Report of Policy Action Team 7*, London: Cabinet Office.

SEU (2001) *A New Commitment to Neighbourhood Renewal: National Strategy Action Plan*, London: Cabinet Office.

Smith, D. (2008) The politics of studentification and '(un)balanced' urban populations: lessons for gentrification and Sustainable Communities?, *Urban Studies*, 45 (12), pp.2541-2564.

Smith, N. (1996) *The New Urban Frontier: Gentrification and the Revanchist City*. London: Routledge.

Society Guardian (2003) Agenda setters, *The Guardian*, 10 September 2003.

Somerville, P. (2004) State rescaling and democratic transformation, *Space and Polity*, 8 (2), pp.137-156.

Sprigings, N., Leather, P. and Nevin, B. (2006) Semi-detached housing market theory for sale: suit first time buyer or investor, *Housing Studies Association conference*, 19-20 April 2006, York.

SQW (2005) *Research into the Housing Aspirations and Perceptions of People Living Outside the South Yorkshire Housing Market Renewal Pathfinder Area*, final report to Transform South Yorkshire, Sheffield: Transform South Yorkshire, available from: http://www.transformsouthyorkshire.org.uk/documents/Final_report_Outseer_Perceptions_Study.pdf [accessed 19 January 2010].

Swyngedouw, E. (1992) The Mammon quest: 'Glocalization', interspatial competition and the monetary order: the construction of new scales, pp.39-67 in: Dunford, M. and Kafkalas, G. (Eds) *Cities and Regions in the New Europe*, London: Belhaven Press.

Syrett, S. and North, D. (2008) *Renewing Neighbourhoods: Work, Enterprise and Governance*, Bristol: Policy Press.

The Guardian (2008) 'Pop goes the property boom', Saturday February 16 2008 p.1 Money news & features.

The Guardian (2009) 'House prices predicted to fall in 2010', Katie Allen in *The Guardian*, Monday 28 December 2009.

Third, H. (1995) *Affordable Childcare and Housing: a Case Study of Tenants of a Black Housing Association*, Findings no. 79, York: Joseph Rowntree Foundation.

Thomas, H. and Imrie, R. (1997) Urban Development Corporations and local governance in the UK, *Tijdschrift voor economische en sociale geografie*, 88 (1), pp.53-64.

Townsend, P. (1979) *Poverty in the United Kingdom: a survey of household resources and standards of living*, Harmondsworth: Penguin Books.

Trickett, L. and Lee, P. (2010 forthcoming) Leadership of 'sub-regional' places in the context of growth, *Policy Studies*.

Trickett, L., Murie, A. and Gibney, J. (Eds) (2008) *Leadership and Place*, Birmingham: Centre for Urban and Regional Studies, University of Birmingham.

Turok, I. and Edge, N. (1999) *The Jobs Gap in Britain's Cities: Employment Loss and Labour Market Consequences*, Bristol: Policy Press.

Uitermark, J. (2002) Rescaling, 'scale fragmentation' and the regulation of antagonistic relationships, *Progress in Human Geography*, 26 (6), pp.743-765.

Urban Living (2004) *Urban Living Prospectus*, submission to the Office of the Deputy Prime Minister, West Bromwich: Urban Living.

Urban Living (2006) *Scheme Update Submission*, West Bromwich: Urban Living, available online at: http://www.urbanliving.org.uk/downloads/Urban%20Living,%20 Scheme%20Update%20Submission%2006.pdf [accessed 27 February 2010].

Urban Task Force (1999) *Towards an Urban Renaissance*, final report of the Urban Task Force, London: Spon.

Urban Task Force (2005) *Towards a Strong Urban Renaissance*, an independent report by members of the Urban Task Force, London: Urban Task Force.

Victorian Society (2006) The Victorian terrace: an endangered species again?, *The Victorian*, 21 March 2006, London: the Victorian Society.

Wallace, A. (2004) *Understanding Local Housing Markets? Examining Approaches to Housing Market Analysis*, ESRC/ODPM postgraduate research programme, working paper 6, London: Office of the Deputy Prime Minister.

Wannop, U. and Cherry, G. E. (1994) The development of regional planning in the UK, *Planning Perspectives*, 9, pp.29-60.

Webster, D. (1998) Employment change, housing abandonment and sustainable development: structural processes and structural issues, in: Lowe, S., Spencer, S. and Keenan, P. (Eds), *Housing abandonment in Britain: studies in the cause and effects of low demand housing*, York: Centre for Housing Policy, University of York.

Williams, G. (2004) *Housing Market Renewal: Local Strategies for Intervention*, presented to the conference of the Association of European Schools of Planning (AESOP), Grenoble, France, 1-3 July 2004.

Willis, B. (2005) HMR forces to cut back demolition, *Regeneration and Renewal*, 2 September 2005, p.9.

Wilson, W. J. (1990) *The Truly Disadvantaged: the Inner City, the Underclass, and Public Policy*, Chicago: University of Chicago Press.

Wolman, H. (1995) Local government institutions and democratic governance, pp.135-159 in: Judge, D., Stoker, G. and Wolman, H. (Eds), *Theories of Urban Politics*, London: Sage.

Wood, M. and Vamplew, C. (1999) *Neighbourhood Images in Teesside* (Findings summary, April 1999), York: Joseph Rowntree Foundation.

Yates J. and Whitehead C. (1998) In defence of greater agnosticism: a response to Galster's "Comparing demand-side and supply-side housing policies", *Housing Studies*, 13 (3), pp.415-423.

Appendix 1: Map of HMR Pathfinders and Growth Areas

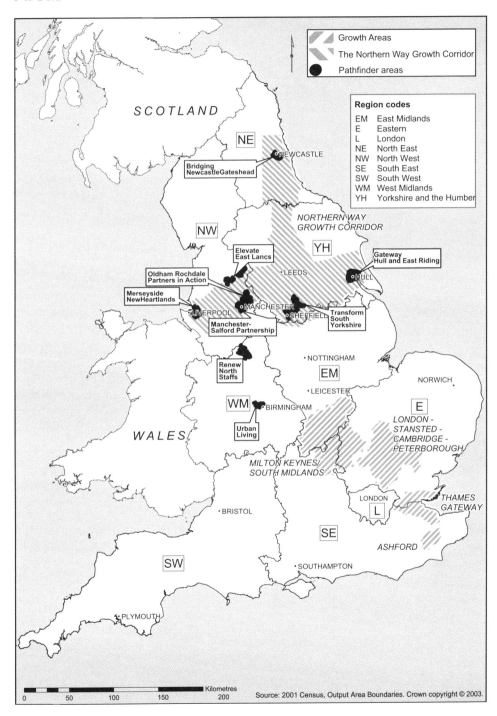

Growth Areas
The Northern Way Growth Corridor
Pathfinder areas

Region codes
EM East Midlands
E   Eastern
L   London
NE North East
NW North West
SE South East
SW South West
WM West Midlands
YH Yorkshire and the Humber

SCOTLAND

NE
Bridging NewcastleGateshead
NEWCASTLE

NORTHERN WAY GROWTH CORRIDOR

NW
Elevate East Lancs
YH
Gateway Hull and East Riding
Oldham Rochdale Partners in Action
LEEDS
HULL
Merseyside NewHeartlands
LIVERPOOL
MANCHESTER
SHEFFIELD
Transform South Yorkshire
Manchester-Salford Partnership
Renew North Staffs
NOTTINGHAM
EM
NORWICH
LEICESTER
WM
BIRMINGHAM
E
Urban Living
LONDON - STANSTED - CAMBRIDGE - PETERBOROUGH
WALES
MILTON KEYNES/ SOUTH MIDLANDS
LONDON
L
THAMES GATEWAY
BRISTOL
SE
ASHFORD
SW
SOUTHAMPTON
PLYMOUTH

Kilometres
0   50   100   150   200

Source: 2001 Census, Output Area Boundaries. Crown copyright © 2003.

Appendix 2: The CURS index of the risk of low and changing demand for housing

In a number of the studies reported in this book the data used are from the 1991 census. A baseline risk indicator is constructed by standardising these variables for census enumeration districts (EDs) using chi-square standardisation, and then summing the standardised values to give an overall risk index. Equal weighting is given to each of the standardised variables.

Thus, in each case:

$$\chi^2 = \frac{(x_o - x_e)^2}{x_e}$$

$$x_{standardised} = \log_{10}\left(\chi^2 + 1\right)$$

and the overall risk index,

$$risk = \sum x_{standardised}$$

for all variables.

The expected proportion of the denominators for each variable is:

Variable	Description	Expected proportion
Age 65+	Proportion of population aged 65+	0.162030
Flat	Proportion of dwelling spaces that are flats	0.115582
Terrace	Proportion of dwelling spaces that are terrace houses	0.310495
Inactive	Proportion of population that is economically inactive	0.198629
Unemployed	Proportion of economically active population that is unemployed	0.109935

Where the standardised score for an ED was negative, it was set to zero. One of the main advantages of the chi-square standardisation method is that it copes well with small area counts because it under-weights the contribution of small counts.

Appendix 3: Adjacency analysis method

A GIS was employed to adjust each unit of statistical geography's crude risk score on the basis of the average scores of surrounding (intersecting) units to mitigate variations in the population size of units. This technique also allowed the identification of coalescences of risk (areas with a large concentration of problems associated with a weakening of demand). In effect, this allows the risk index for one area to be influenced by that of neighbouring areas, in the same way that perceptions of neighbourhood blight, anti-social behaviour and fear of crime might also transcend boundaries.

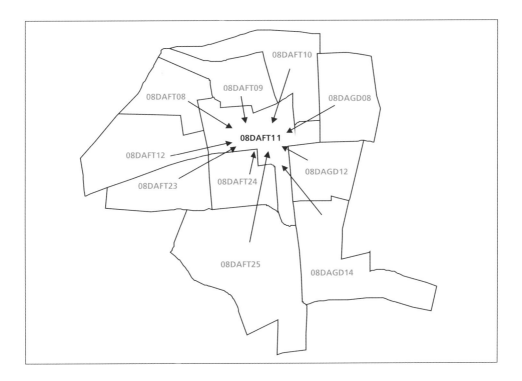

Given the variable size and shape of geographical units, equal weighting was given to each. It was not considered advantageous to introduce an arbitrary decay function or similar on the basis that boundaries, in isolation, randomly describe the properties within them. Any unit that had a negative or zero standardised score prior to averaging was reset to zero. This has the effect of suppressing the 'travel' of low scores into very different adjacent areas, which may be a result of natural obstacles such as rivers, parkland or other physical features such as transport corridors.

Appendix 4: Pathfinder performance reviews

Outputs of the Pathfinders summarised from publically available annual reports of the Pathfinders

Bridging Newcastle-Gateshead (BNG)	2003/04	2004/05	2005/06	2006/07	2007/08	Total
Properties demolished:	388	409	506	258	289	1,850
Private		97	314			411
Social		312	192			504
Properties improved/ refurbished (all)	33	232	433	1,692	1,623	4,013
New homes built		2	0	44	124	170
Dwellings acquired:	98	244	170	115		627
Private	98					98
Land acquired (hectares)	0.3		4.7	1.7	3.8	10.5
Expenditure		£28,000,000	£31,920,000	£23,000,000	£40,910,000	£123,830,000

Source: Bridging NewcastleGateshead annual reports 2003/04-2007/08.
Notes: New homes for BNG includes conversions from 2006/07.

Partners in Action (PiA) Oldham Rochdale	2004/05	2005/06	2006/07	2007/08	Total
Properties demolished:	78	107	161	148	494
Private	19				19
Social	59				59
Properties improved/ refurbished (all)	832	972	278	454	2,536
New homes built		27	106	165	298
Dwellings acquired:	150	224	211	174	759
Private	133				133
Land acquired (hectares)		0.5	1.8	8.1	10.4
Expenditure	£17,150,000	£30,936,001	£30,072,765	£37,410,000	£115,568,766

Source: PiA annual reports 2004/05-2007/08.

Urban Living Birmingham Solihull	2004/05	2005/06	2006/07	2007/08	Total
Properties demolished:	71	306	60	207	644
Private	11	4	0	88	103
Social	60	302	60	119	541
Properties improved/ refurbished (all)	10	6,115	518	2,262	8,905
New homes built	47	62	52	36	197
Dwellings acquired:	554	817	70	167	1,608
Private	104	107	70	132	413
Land acquired (hectares)	9.6	0	1.0	4.5	15.1
Expenditure	£13,648,755	£30,791,000	£15,200,000	£29,210,000	£88,849,755

Source: Urban Living annual reports 2004/05-2007/08.

Renew North Staffordshire	2004-06	2006/07	2007/08	Total
Properties demolished:	296	215	282	793
Private				0
Social				0
Properties improved/ refurbished (all)	1,547	846	3,000	5,393
New homes built			52	52
Dwellings acquired:	363	300	466	1,129
Private				0
Land acquired (hectares)		1.4		1.4
Expenditure	£19,300,000	£29,000,000	£38,410,000	£86,710,000

Source: RENEW annual reports 2005/06-2007/08.

NewHeartlands Merseyside	2004/05	2005/06	2006/07	2007/08	Total
Properties demolished:	132	185	256	338	911
Private	99	137	155	204	595
Social	33	48	101	134	316
Properties improved/ refurbished (all)	2,332	5,383	873	599	9,187
New homes built	6	11	0	0	17
Dwellings acquired:	683	856	393	485	2,417
Private	386	714	288	228	1,616
Land acquired (hectares)	8.8	3.0	0.2	0.8	12.8
Expenditure	£34,350,000	£51,700,000	£46,800,000	£50,810,000	£183,660,000

Source: NewHeartlands annual reports 2004/05-2007/08.
Notes: New homes in 2004/05, 2005/06 for NewHeartlands includes 'constructed or converted'; total number of homes refurbished for 2004/05 includes non-HMRI funded properties; acquired dwellings is 'total no. of properties acquired for Pathfinder purposes'; new homes in 2005/06: 321 were built without HMR grant, but on land acquired by the Pathfinder; refurbished properties are identified under a separate line in 2006/07 annual report as 'all homes refurbished that are financed wholly or partly by HMRF'; properties demolished or refurbished in 2007/08 are wholly or in part HMR funded.

Gateway Hull and East Riding	2005/06	2006/07	2007/08	Total
Properties demolished:	147	92	92	147
Private	32	78		32
Social	115	14		115
Properties improved/ refurbished (all)	0	20	332	0
New homes built		44	100	
Dwellings acquired:	75	146	221	75
Private				0
Land acquired (hectares)	0.3	7.4	0	0.3
Expenditure	£8,700,000	£16,300,000	£24,900,000	£8,700,000

Source: Gateway annual reports 2005/06-2007/08.
Note: New build for Gateway in includes conversions.

Elevate East Lancashire	2004/05	2005/06	2006/07	2007/08	Total
Properties demolished: Private Social	384	331	309	272	1,296
Properties improved/ refurbished (all)	674	830	336	506	2,346
New homes built	428	336	244	249	1,257
Dwellings acquired: Private	596	449	454	384	1,883
Land acquired (hectares)	5.4	1.5	1.4		8.3
Expenditure	£22,840,000	£43,160,000	£46,000,000	£48,810,000	£160,810,000

Source: Elevate East Lancashire annual reports 2004/05-2007/08
Note: Figures for 2004/05 are reported for 'the Pathfinder area'; new build include conversions and in 2005/06 includes private housing on HMR acquired land.

Transform South Yorkshire	2004-06	Total
Properties demolished:	1,732	1,732
Private	130	130
Social	1,602	1,602
Properties improved/refurbished (all)	1,915	1,915
New homes built	1,915	1,915
Environmental works – homes affected	8,802	8,802
Homes involved in masterplanning process	189,489	189,489
Homes subject to additional management measures (neighbourhood wardens)	32,074	32,074
Expenditure	£43,941,512	£43,941,512

Source: TSY annual report 2005/06.
Note: Demolished properties include all properties demolished within the Pathfinder area.

Manchester-Salford Partnership	2005/06	2006/07	2007/08	Total
Properties demolished: Private Social	1,701	755	381	2,837
Properties improved/ refurbished (all)	8,023	2,305	512	10,840
New homes built	4,312	3,267	3,371	10,950
Dwellings acquired: Private	1,855	601	540	2,996
Land acquired (hectares)	23.0	8.6	15.8	47.4
Expenditure	£82,011,720	£52,047,000	£53,626,339	£187,685,059

Source: MSP annual reports 2004/05-2007/08.
Note: New homes include all properties built on Pathfinder land.

Index